When is my Daddy Coming Home

This is a story of strength, heartache, an unfathomable will to live, and above all, it's a testament to love and dedication

ANNIE WARREN

Copyright © 2024 by Annie Warren

All rights reserved. No part of this book may be reproduced or transmitted in any form or by any means, electronic or mechanical, including photocopying, recording, or by any information storage and retrieval system, without permission in writing from the copyright owner.

Australian Self Publishing Group, Pty. Ltd / Inspiring Publishers
PO Box 159, Calwell, ACT 2905
Australia. Phone: 61-(0) 2 6291-2904
http://australianselfpublishinggroup.com

Member of the:
Australian Publishers Association.
International Book Publishing Association.
The Small Press Network

Author: Annie Warren

Title: **WHEN IS MY DADDY COMING HOME**
This is a story of strength, heartache, an unfathomable will to live, and above all, it's a testament to love and dedication

ISBN: 978-1-923250-25-3 (print)
ISBN: 978-1-923250-26-0 (ePub2)

Bob's Story

In 1976, Bob and I had been married for a year and were about to embark on a working holiday around Australia. Our close friends, Agnes, Jack, and their children, Cathy aged 10 and Jimmy 6, had been spending weekends exploring our beautiful, picturesque coastline and enjoying 4-wheel driving adventures along the beaches. We thought it would be great fun to expand our day trips and explore all around Australia.

Jack ran his own concreting business, and Bob worked for him. They were both excellent at their jobs and had no trouble finding work. They both had the gift of the gab, so there were always plenty of tales to share. We weren't entirely sure if all their stories were true, however they never failed to entertain us, and we shared many laughs.

There was plenty of work available in the 70s, and both Jack and Bob were versatile enough to tackle various jobs. So, after one of our weekend adventures, we made the decision to each purchase a caravan and become 'Carnies,' as our kids would later call us.

Bob and I set off first, heading out to Bathurst, Orange, and Dubbo, picking up jobs along the way. We worked at meat works, pubs, cleaning gigs, and even did some concreting while exploring each area. It was incredibly exciting, with so much to see and countless people to meet along the way. Our van was only 16 feet long, quite comfortable, although not as luxurious as the ones you see today. There were no gas or diesel heaters, nor showers or toilets in them. I remember one exceptionally chilly night when we invited a young couple, who only had a 2-man nylon tent, to share our van. They slept on the seating area which was certainly cosier and much warmer than their tent. They were grateful we invited them into the van that night as it ended up snowing, and they would have frozen if they had stayed in their tent.

The next morning, we decided to pack up and hightail it north in search of warmer weather.

We met up with Jack and Agnes and settled around the Yeppoon-Rockhampton area. Agnes home-schooled Cathy and Jim while the rest of us searched for work. I ended up with a job packing meat, which I despised. Coming from a background in pharmacy, it was quite a change. I decided to leave as soon as I could find another job, but for the time being, we needed the money as our funds were running low.

The boys scored most of their work from the local pub, which they affectionately dubbed their office. It was networking at its finest. Forget LinkedIn, back in those days, the barstool was their LinkedIn profile pic, and a schooner in hand was their resume! That's also where I snagged my next job, in the bistro and behind the bar. I loved the people and the experience.

Life back then was one perpetual holiday - the days were filled with fishing, crabbing, the endless shuffle of playing cards and board games. No screens to distract us, no virtual worlds to escape to - just good old-fashioned fun under the sun! It was such a simple life with no real pressure, it was all we knew and we were having fun.

We got involved in the local football club and as their main fundraiser, Bob suggested he cook a traditional Māori Hangi. He had spent time in New Zealand a few years before and loved the food. It turned out to be huge. They dug holes in the park, had a roaring fire with the river rocks falling into the hole and baskets of food which were wrapped in banana leaves all being buried and looking like warm graves in the local park. A lot more people turned up than expected as word had spread around about these crazy guys doing a Hangi and they ran out of food. While many people were disappointed, those who were fed loved it, and a significant amount of money was raised.

Our time was running out and sadly it was time to say goodbye to the Capricorn area. So, after about 6 months we headed north again where Jack and Agnes were to meet us around Townsville. Bob got his next job at the meat works, however I felt sick just thinking about working there and for good reason. That's when I realised we were expecting our first child. Our life was about to change forever.

We were so excited! Daniel was born in March 1978 and he was perfect. Sharna came along in June 1980 and our family was complete.

We traded in our little 16-foot caravan and bought a 27-foot caravan then moved just north of Townsville where Bob found work at the nickel plant. We made many friends. Beth and Wayne, Lee and Steve, Elaine, Annette, Gary and many more. We are still good friends with some today.

We explored the area about one hour north of Townsville around Crystal Creek, Bluewater and Rollingstone. We were always camping and cooling off in the rivers, creeks and waterfalls. Crystal Creek, Paluma, and Hidden Valley were a favourite. We had some friends living up the mountains at Hidden Valley and another couple who bought the local Telephone Exchange/Post Office/Mail Run and Fuel Depot. They were always looking for people to help manage their business so they could go on holidays back to Europe to visit family.

That's where I came in. Myself and the kids, now aged 5 and 3, offered to run their business while they were away. Bob would join us when he had time off work. The Telephone Exchange was the old peg board style, a party line where every family had a different ring: 4 short, 2 long; 2 long, 1 short, etc. You had to listen for the rings and anyone could listen in on the conversations. You never spoke badly or gossiped about people, as it got back to them very quickly. There were no secrets in the mountains!

The only fuel available was in 44-gallon drums so the men had to manoeuvre them onto their trucks themselves. With no access to modern conveniences, generators provided our only power source. You really do miss the luxuries of modern living when you don't have them. Cooking and illuminating our nights posed early challenges, but we adapted swiftly, mastering the art of firing up the generators before dusk stole our daylight. It was like stepping back in time with no modern luxuries, no traffic, no mobile phones or internet, computers, electric toothbrushes or hair dryers.

Heating water meant lighting the donkey heater each day, a familiar task from my childhood. The children, resourceful as ever, took on their roles, gathering twigs and branches to ignite the flames. I can't remember fire starters being around in those days, though they probably were. Dan loved the fire and took pride in tending to the flames. Not that we needed hot showers as it was usually pretty hot up there and we did a lot of swimming in the refreshing mountain waterfalls.

The post box and mail run were really interesting. Every Friday I drove an hour to Paluma and picked up the mail for Hidden

Valley. Hidden Valley was a tiny town. It had a school, tennis court, a few houses, a post box, fuel and telephone exchange. On mail day the mountain truly came alive. From every winding dirt track, residents emerged, creating a bustling scene that belied the town's remote location. It was a revelation to witness how many people called these mountains home, each one hidden away in their own secluded corner of the world.

Returning from Paluma, I'd dive into sorting the mail, knowing for many locals this was their lifeline to the outside world. Once the mail was sorted, the kids and I would embark on our next adventure: a 4-hour round trip delivering the mail to the stations. Along with the mail, we carried essentials like milk, bread and any other necessities they needed until their next trip to town. They were eager for a chat, and a refreshing cup of tea or cool drink was always ready for us. What a wonderful experience it was and we loved going up to help them out.

I remember someone had organised a friendly cricket match to raise money for a family in need, only there wasn't a cricket ground. So, the locals started clearing a spot of unused bushland. However, there were a few tree stumps in the middle of the pitch that proved difficult to remove. Bob managed to get his hands on a few sticks of dynamite and decided to blow them out. It was quite a spectacle for the sleepy mountain village, but, lo and behold, it did the trick and we had a cricket pitch. It is quite amazing what happens in these remote mountain communities, and what equipment turns up for use.

In 1982, Bob landed a new job working in a Sugar Mill an hour south of Townsville in a small town called Giru. After a few months in the caravan park outside of town, we sold our caravan and rented a 3-bedroom house on a cane farm for $40 per week. Giru was a tight-knit community where everyone knew one another. Nearly everyone worked at the sugar mill, picked fruit, vegetables, or packed mangoes at the local factory. As the work was seasonal, in the off-season Bob would find alternate work in mines, quarries or the local mango farm.

After getting married on the Central Coast of NSW and embarking on our working trip, we discovered that we enjoyed the warm winters in North Queensland. We never anticipated staying for 13 years as the summers could be intensely hot. However, once the kids came along, it just happened. They started school and joined team sports, making their own friends. The relaxed lifestyle suited us, and we settled in.

We had a wonderful group of friends with whom we socialised, camping, fishing, playing tennis, touch football, barbecues, card games, and hosting kids' sleepovers. Life was busy and fulfilling, and we loved it that way. We had two dogs, a cat, ducks, lots of chickens, and Swampy, the pet baby kangaroo whom we saved after his mum was killed on the road. Bob was always bringing home an animal or someone in need of care or a good feed.

Bob, a dedicated gardener, tended to all our vegetable needs. Our garden flourished under his care, boasting a diverse array of produce including corn, peas, carrots, potatoes, pumpkin, beans, capsicums, celery, herbs, and more. In addition to our main garden, Bob maintained a second plot, securely fenced off and reserved for his most prized plants: chillis, onions, and special "tomato" varieties. It became the children's responsibility to safeguard this sanctuary from any wandering chickens.

Bob cultivated his own chillis and onions, crafting a potent jar of pickled chillis. Positioned high on the top shelf, beyond children's reach, it boasted a prominent skull and crossbones, with the word 'POISON' emblazoned across it. Proudly presented on social occasions and after a few drinks, it became a centrepiece for challenging each other's masculinity among the gathered men.

Bob's creativity knew no bounds. He was an exceptional artist and he enjoyed painting Disney characters on the water tank alongside the children. His talents extended to leatherwork, creating stubby coolers, belts, hats, and handbags. A master of wit and bullshit, he effortlessly spun funny little poems for the kids' school projects, somewhat inappropriate, but all the kids loved the poems and the teachers were certainly entertained.

Christmas was always an exciting time spent with friends we considered family. For our final Christmas and New Year together, we spent a week of festivities on Magnetic Island with the Croattos and Readings. We rented Mini Mokes to explore the island, enjoyed swimming, played charades, relaxed, and celebrated the end of 1987 while looking forward to the new year and all the exciting possibilities it may bring.

When Is My Daddy Coming Home

It was early 1988. Bob had been working away as a fly in, fly out driller with the mines at Croydon. He missed the kids terribly, so he decided to come back home and find local work. Work was easy to come by in the 80's, and being a jack of all trades, he didn't have trouble picking up a job. He seemed to enjoy the drilling work and managed to secure a position with a Quarrying Company just north of Bowen.

Mornings were chaos as we hustled to prepare and make it to the bus stop in time. Daniel had just turned 10 and Sharna was 7. They attended the small local school in Giru, a short 4-kilometre journey away, where they were among only 62 other students enrolled. I volunteered at the tuck shop, commonly known these days as the canteen, where I had the pleasure of getting to know every child by name. It was such a friendly little community, always ready to lend a hand when needed.

Bob and I also coached the soccer team, which took Grades 4, 5, 6 and 7 to make one team. It was funny as we had shy little kids and then tall confident grade 6 & 7 kids all mixed in together. The field was hard and dry, there was no green grass and it was full of bindis and cats' eyes. They were tough kids and tried not to fall over too often. They didn't win many games, however we all had fun and lots of laughs and being in a team sport was a wonderful experience.

Annie Warren

It was a lovely Thursday morning, bright and sunny as the weather settled after the long, hot summer that Townsville is known for. On the 28 of April, 1988, like any other typical morning, I woke to find a cup of tea on my bedside table. I didn't even hear his motor bike start up.

After returning from dropping the kids off at the bus stop and getting organised for my day, I heard a loud knock on the door. Not expecting anyone to visit, I was quite shocked by the knocking. It was the local policeman, whom we knew well as we played touch football with him, so I wasn't concerned by his presence. He asked if Bob was home or still working away, and then he said, "Please tell me he is still away!"

That's when I became deeply concerned. The policeman informed me that there had been an accident at the turnoff to the quarry where Bob had started working. He had only been working at this Drilling job for 9 days. Bob would ride his motorbike to Home Hill where he would leave it at the service station and then catch a lift in the work ute. He had only just met the driver a few days before. Apparently, as they reached the work site and turned into the quarry, the sun blinded the driver who did not see the fully loaded semi-trailer bearing down on their work ute. Bob's side of the ute took the full impact and the ute ended up in a paddock.

That's when your heart stops for a few beats and life changes forever.

The policeman stayed with me until we received a phone call informing us where Bob would be taken. If he had spinal injuries, they would fly him to Brisbane; otherwise, he would be transported to Townsville. The wait was agonising and it felt like hours not knowing what to expect. Everyone's life was so busy, so I did not call any friends to come and be with me, and I had no family members who lived nearby. I thought I would be ok. Oh, how silly I was, I was so naive, but at that moment, we didn't yet know the extent of his injuries. I had my bags packed and was ready to fly to Brisbane just in case.

Little did I know what lay ahead of me, and my goodness, you could never prepare yourself for what we were about to experience. Our two kids. What should I tell them? Bob had come home so we could be a family, not a distant partner or father.

The phone call came through after several hours, he was being taken by helicopter to Townsville. I was so relieved and thankful as it would make my life a lot easier with the kids, school, accommodation, friends, all our animals, and transport, etc. I went to the school and explained to Dan and Sharna that dad had been in an accident and told them to go home with some friends. I assured them that I would see them later and tell them more about their dad. We had a wonderful group of friends in this little town, and I could never have survived without their support. Robbie, Estelle, Kim and Robyn were wonderful.

I had a little job, house cleaning and caring for an elderly lady. It was something I could do while the kids were at school and be home for them when they arrived home. I was supposed to work that day and gratefully, the lady who I cleaned and worked for drove me to Townsville hospital and stayed with me for several hours. She was so supportive. Thea, I thank you, you have no idea how much I needed you that day.

We arrived at the hospital before Bob as he had to go to Bowen hospital and have X-rays to check for spinal injuries. We sat at the hospital for hours. No one came near us or provided us with updates. The medical staff were busy taking X-rays and fixing his broken body; however, the lack of communication was making me extremely worried and very stressed. I focused on knowing he was alive.

Finally, a nurse sat with me and explained what was going on. She drew a stick figure on a notepad and pointed out the broken bones. There were 21 in total. How do you survive and heal with so many broken bones? He also had a dislocated left shoulder, a deep gash to the head, and the kneecap on his right leg was missing. He was in surgery and they were trying to mend his broken body. On the stick figure, the nurse pointed out that the left arm was fractured 3 times, as was the right leg, the wrist on the right arm was having a plate put in, and his right hip was also dislocated. I think I may have blacked out myself as I couldn't take it all in.

On top of all of that, he also had head trauma and was in a coma. Bob being in a comatose state didn't really concern me at this point as the pain would have been horrendous. I sat outside the ICU all day. It would have to be one of the longest days of my life.

The police report revealed he was not supposed to survive as when they arrived at the scene they said, "No hope given to the passenger. Let's get the driver out". However, the driver died at the scene. Such finality for the driver and the young family he left behind. With all that was going on in my world, I never got to meet the driver or speak with his wife, but I heard he had several children. My heart broke for them. As numb as I was, I still remember thinking how blessed we were to still have Bob here - broken bones will heal. How naive I was to the journey that lay ahead of us.

Thankfully I had organised the children to be picked up and cared for. We had no family up in North Queensland. Our friends became family to us and boy did I need them now, I only had to ask and they were there. Every day they supported me, either at the hospital or picking up Dan and Sharna from school. I appreciated everything they did for us and will never forget the support they gave me.

Comatose

The doctors explained how important it was for Bob to come out of the coma and the sooner the better. After 48 hours brain damage is expected and the longer he stays comatose the more severe it would be. I knew nothing about being in a coma and I was so naive about this whole situation. I was just 36 and my whole life had been turned upside down in an instant. I came home exhausted from the hospital, picked up the kids and we all cuddled and cried together. I rang my family and Bob's sister, telling them about the accident and not knowing from one minute to the next what was going to happen, but will keep them informed.

The revolving door of doctors, the constant changing of dressings, the tireless efforts to coax him out of the coma - it was all consuming. Each day brought new challenges and more operations. The weight of it all was exhausting, just being there, bearing witness to the struggle, and then having to repeatedly recount the day's events to concerned friends and family.

The kids were so confused their dad wasn't coming home and wouldn't be for a long time. Trying to protect them and just tell them what I thought they could handle and what they needed to know was difficult to manage. It didn't help that I was spending every minute at the hospital and coming home tired and exhausted.

Every day we were hit with more devastating news: 4 breaks on one leg alone, 5-hour long operations and severe head injuries.

He developed breathing difficulties, so they put him on a ventilator. A tracheostomy was inserted into his throat to help him breathe, but an extremely high temperature was also playing havoc with his condition. The reality was starting to set in as was the emotional exhaustion.

Brian, my brother, flew up from the Central Coast on the 3rd of May, 5 days after the accident and what a relief it was to see a family member and what a godsend he was. There was so much to do - Workers' compensation forms, union reps, Social Security (known as Centrelink these days), solicitors, doctors, social workers - the list went on and every minute of our days was taken.

My mind was like a fog; nothing was clear or seemed to make sense. I watched lips moving, words spilling out, but I couldn't absorb any more. It was as if I had reached a saturation point, my senses overwhelmed by the constant barrage of information and emotion. Every minute felt consumed by the relentless march of responsibilities, leaving me adrift in a haze of exhaustion and confusion.

The doctors spoke to Brian alone and told him of their concern: Bob would never be able to live a normal life and they didn't expect him to survive very long.

Back into surgery to have pins and a plate put in his right arm, plaster on his left leg and metal bars sticking out of his right leg - how much more could he endure? I was beside myself, so scared. They told me he could be in this comatose state for months. How can you sleep for so long? Can he hear me? Does he know my voice? Does he even know we are there? Although, in the condition his body was in, why would you want to wake up?

I was pretty impressed with the doctors and hospital for fixing all of Bob's broken limbs, as I've since learnt that not all hospitals do that when the patient is not expected to survive.

The doctors needed the bed in the ICU, so they decided to move him to a ward. However, no specific ward wanted to accept him with the significant amount of injuries he had: head trauma, comatose, multiple fractured limbs, a missing kneecap, plates, screws, breathing difficulties - the list was never-ending.

Mary the Social Worker became a tower of strength for me, organising appointments with workers compensation, looking into Nursing Homes and helping me try to understand what was happening. She was the one that stepped forward when all the wards were arguing about where Bob should go and worked on finding a suitable solution. Finally, he went to the Orthopaedic Ward, but we had to change his doctor to the Deputy Superintendent. No doctor wanted the responsibility; there were too many injuries. We felt like a yoyo getting passed back and forth and no one taking a stand of responsibility.

The money stopped that day as Bob had only been at this job for 9 days. He came home to be with his family after the fly in fly out job. He realised how much he missed the family, and the kids were missing him also. There was no holiday pay or long service, the money just stopped. The company never contacted me and never has to this day, which really pissed me off. It's not like he was at fault, he was the passenger in a work ute going to work. I am still shocked by that today, their lack of concern or empathy for my family. Apparently, the boss was following the work ute a few cars behind, so he was one of the first to arrive at the accident and was able to name the victims.

A gesture from the kids' school, with its mere 62 pupils, touched us deeply. Their donation of $192 for petrol was more than just a sum of money; it was a symbol of their support and care during our time of need. In the 80s, such an amount held significant weight, especially considering the distance - a round trip of approximately 120 kilometres to the hospital. We were truly grateful for their contribution, knowing that it would help ease the burden of travel during those trying times.

My sister Liz arrived on the 16th of May after leaving the Central Coast NSW by McCafferty's bus, a 36-hour trip, leaving behind a husband and 3 teenage boys. What a mission for her, and what she was about to walk into. We were told to make arrangements for Bob to go into a Nursing Home as there had been no improvements, no response and no change. Were they kidding? It had only been 3 weeks! I was in total shock.

4 weeks in, Bob seemed to have had enough. His knee and shin were infected, arms were stiffening and there was no sign of his eyes responding. His stomach was expanding and after dye was put through, they found his bowel was breaking down. He looked so uncomfortable.

Then he took a turn for the worse and we were told he was going to die within a few hours. All his organs were shutting down and only his heart was working, 3 times its normal rate and producing too many toxins for his body to manage. It was just a matter of time now; he couldn't cope like this for any length of time. Watching him was so exhausting for us also.

I was advised to send for the kids so they could say goodbye to their dad. No child should ever have to be confronted with what they saw and had to do. The look on their little faces was terrifying. All they wanted was their Dad back to his normal, cheeky self. No mum should ever have to tell a 10 and 7 year old that their dad was about to die. It was the hardest thing I have ever done.

He continued for hours, his heart racing, the doctors still giving him no hope, only a matter of time. Liz and I were told to go to the Red Cross House just across the road and get some rest, as we were exhausted. Like we could sleep! We were expecting to get a call at any moment. But we didn't. And none of us knew the fight to live that Bob Warren had.

The next morning, not knowing what to expect as we walked in the room, there was Bob, breathing normally and looking very peaceful. The doctors are still telling us he cannot survive with the amount of toxins his body was producing. He would die within the next 2 days. This period was a nightmare, a waiting game, a not knowing game and a game that changed every hour, every minute, every day and every week. No one knew what the outcome would be.

He fooled the doctors once again and didn't die in those 2 days.

After about 3-4 months he seemed to move his left leg when touched and became more alert. Was this a sign he was coming out of the comatose state? But then it would stop. How can someone just lay asleep for so long? I wanted to shake him, I was so angry he was just sleeping, and he looked so relaxed and peaceful while I was so beyond exhaustion.

At 18 weeks, we were so elated to reach a positive milestone: he squeezed my hand on demand for the first time. After being in a coma for what felt like eternity, a sense of relief washed over me, seeing him finally break through the veil of unconsciousness. It was a flicker of light in the darkness.

My family was a fabulous support also, they all felt so helpless, being so far away. Every family member came and supported me, leaving behind their own families. Some by plane, others by bus, which was a very long trip. I needed and appreciated everything they did.

The support wasn't only necessary during our time at the hospital. Upon returning home in the evenings, there were animals to feed, laundry to do, shopping, cooking, spending time with the kids, and then attempting to process the events of the day. And the phone never seemed to stop ringing. Just remember, no one had a mobile phone in 1988. What were they? They would have certainly made life a lot easier back then. Instead, we had a phone attached to the wall, not even hands-free. I'd stand in the same spot, recounting the same story over and over again to everyone who called. Some managed to cope with what we shared, while others were such a mess that we had to comfort them. Each night, we all collapsed into bed exhausted, only to face it all again the next day.

The doctors and the hospital were putting pressure on us. They needed his bed; all the broken limbs were now mended as best they could be; it was time to go into a Nursing Home. His tendons were contracting in the wrists, elbows, legs, arms and hands - this is when the muscles and tissues in the body shrink and tighten up, making it difficult to move or straighten the affected limb, or in Bob's case, limbs. He was not responding to physiotherapy, and his future didn't look very promising. He needed special splints made up. The medical staff were still giving him a slight chance of coming out of the coma.

Bob then started to show slow, subtle movements in his right foot and we noticed he was starting to respond when we spoke to him. We discovered if we asked simple yes or no questions, he was able to respond by slightly lifting his right foot for yes and lowering it for no. Additionally, he started to display a slight movement in his right forearm. These gestures spoke volumes, bridging the gap between his silent world and our longing for understanding, offering us all a glimmer of hope.

A suggestion was made to take him to Sydney and try to get him into a rehabilitation ward. Mary, my social worker, supported this idea and started approaching the doctors, completing paperwork and researching suitable facilities. She was truly incredible, and what an undertaking it would have been. The doctors filled out all the forms for him to go to a rehabilitation hospital in Sydney.

At 21 weeks we received a call saying Bob had been accepted at an Annexe hospital until they could assess him. We needed to show them there was hope while he waited for a bed. The hospital would pay for the transfer until a court case was heard and his doctor and nurse would have to travel down with him. He was to leave in about 3 weeks.

I was told to keep an account of every cent I spent and they would reimburse me. It soon added up, all the fuel I used travelling the 120km round trip to the hospital - 5 times a week, chemist bills, disabled needs, special clothes, his skin was dry and scaly so special soaps and oils, plane and bus tickets, lamb's wool, etc.

We even had to find where he left his motorbike and have it returned so we could sell it before we left. There was so much to do.

Moving Bob to Sydney meant we also had to go. We had to pack up a house and find a removalist. It would be a very long trip driving from Townsville down to Sydney with the kids. I would need to enrol the kids in a new school. No-one was looking forward to this journey, especially me.

When is my Daddy Coming Home

We had to leave all our wonderful friends, who had been there every minute of every day, looking after my two kids, feeding us, taking them to sports, fixing my car, the list is endless. So, to Robbie, Estelle, Kim, Robyn, Wailsea, Ronnie, Ian, Thea and family – thank you! I could never have managed without you all.

Sydney, Here We Come

Bob was scheduled to fly down to Sydney with his doctor and nurse accompanying him. They had to remove 10 seats from the plane to accommodate his bed. It was a massive mission to transport him, ensuring the right people were meeting him at the other end and he went to the right hospital. And on top of all that, hoping he would withstand the journey. I was sick with worry. But there was no time to dwell as I had so much to plan for the kids and myself.

On October 6th, 1988, my sister Liz arrived at 4.45am after the long bus trip from the Central Coast. She was an absolute blessing. Bob was flying out the next day at 11am and we had to be at the airport to see him go. There were so many emotions. Will he survive the trip down? When and where will I see him again? I remember driving home from the hospital after saying goodbye when I was pulled over for speeding; I probably shouldn't have been behind the wheel in my emotional state.

We now had to pack up all our belongings and clean the house. Our little family had lived in this town for 6 years, it was all the kids had known and it was such an emotional time leaving their friends, sport, work and school behind. It was so hard to leave, however Bob's health was my priority. I didn't think I had any tears left in me, but they certainly flowed that day, we even had to leave our beloved dog Boof behind. Thanks to Robyn for taking him.

When is my Daddy Coming Home

After saying our final, emotional goodbyes and driving out of Giru, I was trying to control my tears and comfort the kids when I realised I still had the house key and we had to turn around and head back into town.

No words came for many kilometres along our trip. There was a sniffle and a few sobs, but otherwise just the quietness of us all trying to cope with the next stage we were about to be faced with. And then there was also Dan, who, with every bridge we crossed would say "Are there crocodiles in that water Aunty Liz?". That always put a smile on our face.

I remember as we were driving along, Liz looked at me and asked. "Do you have any plans of where you are going to live?". Wow! I had organised everything except the kids and I. Getting Bob brought down was a huge task and it went so well. The annexe hospital where he was going was organised, the removalists were on their way, the good-byes were done, and the trip down was going well.

But no, I hadn't thought of us. She just looked at me and said, "You can move in with us". I still get teary when I think about that question. I love you sis!

It was a long drive, staying at Mackay, Mundubbera, Brisbane, Muswellbrook then onto the last leg to the Central Coast. My sister Glenys lived in Brisbane, so we stopped in there for 2 days and had some quality time with her family and gave the kids some space to run around. Everyone was so kind and generous; I suppose they felt so sorry for us.

I enrolled the kids into Budgewoi School and what a terribly scary day that was. I went there when I was a kid also, although being one of the first pupils when it opened it wasn't very big. Now there were over 1200 students enrolled and coming from a school with only 62 kids and everyone knowing each other, it was terrifying standing at the assembly looking down on the sea of people and not knowing one single person. My heart sank for them but there was no other choice. I remember Dan saying, "I am not staying here".

As the kids had started school when they were 4, the principal wanted to put them back a year. It was nearly the end of the year and no way in the world was Dan repeating a year of school. He didn't like school that much and wasn't planning on spending any longer there than he had to. After some negotiations, thankfully they were permitted to stay in the same grade. They settled in surprisingly well and made good friends, whom they are still mates with today more than 30 years later.

Now it was time for me to see how Bob was settling in.

The Annexe Hospital

Bob was in an Annex of The Rehabilitation Hospital and about 80 kms away from the Central Coast, all on a very busy freeway. I hadn't seen him now for about 3 weeks, so I was anxious to see any improvements. Before he left Townsville, they had been getting him out of bed and putting him in a very comfy chair. He was also communicating with slight foot movements for yes and no, so I was excited to see what improvements he had made since he arrived in Sydney.

I knew the trip down would probably set him back a little and I wasn't expecting a lot of improvements, after all it had only been 3 weeks. So, my first visit was extremely disappointing, there was no response at all, he was very sleepy and he didn't even know we were there.

The doctors tried to block off his tracheostomy. It was so horrific watching him trying to breathe for the first time through his nose. He went for 13 minutes then he got so distressed and so did I. They had to stop blocking his tracheostomy and try another time.

After another 10 days there was still no improvement, each visit was so distressing and disappointing. Bob was not responding. We found him very quiet, groggy, not bathed and he had an infection in the tracheostomy. There were pressure sores on the big toe and ankle, so we had to do something fast. He was losing weight rapidly - he was now 49kg.

The Rehabilitation Hospital wasn't even looking at taking him until there was some improvement. They were very busy and there were so many people on the waitlist. We had fought too hard for him to just go straight into a nursing home. All our effort seemed like a waste of time and energy. We had tried so hard to get more for him, and this was a huge setback.

After a doctor's meeting I found out they had increased his valium to sedate him. I was furious. This was the opposite of what we were hoping for. We wanted him fully brought out of the coma and stimulated, not sedated. We had to get the doctors on our side.

After cutting back on the medication that he had been administered, and successfully taking the tracheostomy out, very slight improvements started. We got smiles, he started eating small amounts of food, about 5-10 teaspoons of custard and blended meals. The foot movements for yes and no communication had not returned, however Bob started communicating with his eyes, blinking once for yes and twice for no. He started recognising people. It was wonderful when he saw the kids and knew who they were. At long last we were hopeful of getting him into the right facility.

In December 1988, eight months after his accident, the doctors assessed Bob and agreed that he would be accepted to The Rehabilitation Hospital. However, there were no beds available until the New Year. I was thrilled; however, it was still early days and there was a lot to organise.

The paperwork we needed to fill out seemed endless and no one appeared to understand or care about what we were going through. Social Security (now called Centrelink) had stopped the pension for both Bob and I, as Workers Compensation had paid us out in a lump sum of $31,471.24 instead of fortnightly payments.

I had to make that last for many months as well as supply everything for Bob, run my car, cover fuel and repairs, and feed and support two kids. I was so grateful we could live with my sister Liz and her family.

The insurance company had yet to accept responsibility for determining fault in the accident. They attempted to claim that Bob wasn't wearing a seat belt; any reason to evade taking full responsibility for the claim. Two insurance companies were involved: one for the work ute and one for the semi-trailer. It was tough and consumed my life — in fact, I didn't have a life with all this heartache.

The Neurology Board determined that:

1. Bob was incapacitated for work due to the accident.

2. Incapacity is permanent.

3. The nature of the disability is diffuse brain damage.

4. The extent of the disability is 100% loss of bodily function.

We knew by now his future and ours would be full of heartache and pain and would never be easy again.

I had to find solicitors in NSW and still keep the ones in Townsville. It was difficult dealing with both teams. Townsville seemed to put all the paperwork in the too hard basket. This case was too big for them. They didn't answer phone calls. We asked for money to be released to buy Bob a wheelchair and as the two insurance companies involved wouldn't accept responsibility, no money would be released. I had to fight for everything. I just wanted to make his life easier and more comfortable for him. They were not fighting hard enough for us.

There were always doctors, physiotherapists or social workers to see. There were several more operations to have. The nasal tube had to be put back in. We never knew what would greet us when we walked through the door.

I had also applied for a Housing Commission home on the coast and was knocked back because I could live with my sister. There were more needy people out there, so they told me.

The Rehabilitation Hospital

In February 1989, Bob, now 45, was transferred from the Annex Hospital to the Rehabilitation Hospital in Sydney. At this point, he was awake but couldn't speak (anarthria), and it was hard to measure how well he understood things. We had simple eye blinking to communicate for yes and no. He had an impaired gag and swallow reflex, meaning he had trouble swallowing, and had to be fed through a tube in his nose (nasal-gastric feeding). There was a spastic quadriparesis with limited movement present in the upper limbs and there was marked flexion contractions present in both elbows, hips, knees and ankles (his arms and legs were stiff and weak, with limited movement, and his elbows, hips, knees, and ankles were bent inward).

Doctors feel he may have taken a fit and started medication for epilepsy. He was prescribed an x-ray on his swallowing, making sure that food was not going into his lungs. His reflectors were very slow when food was put on his tongue, so we needed to be very careful he didn't choke. We were instructed to only give him thickened fluids, like custard, blended food or thickened drinks, and small amounts to start with. At long last he seemed to be having the right treatment, where the doctors explained his condition and how we could help him.

He was very frail, weighing only 48kg so we needed to build the throat muscles up to help him learn to swallow. This was a very slow process and it took ages for him to swallow each mouthful. We introduced small amounts of food which they recommended. He seemed to really enjoy eating; it must have been wonderful after nearly 10 months of not tasting anything except glycerin swabs in his mouth. Although we didn't know if he even had any taste senses left.

Bob was now fully out of the coma, appearing much more alert responding to flash cards with colours, words, pictures and animals. He enjoyed listening to music and watching old westerns and sports on TV. His eye contact was good.

Finger pointing with the pointer finger on his right hand was working well. His hearing seemed good. He responded to ice on his legs. It was lovely to see some improvements finally after 9-10 months.

As Bob was still not gaining enough weight, we were advised he would need the nasal tube taken out and a feeding gastrostomy tube inserted into his stomach, through which liquid food would be administered as he wasn't getting enough orally with the supplementary oral blended food. This procedure had to be done at a specialist hospital in Sydney, which was becoming a second home to us now.

The gastrostomy tube was horrible, the stomach acid would burn all around the peg sight, resulting in pain and redness that needed regular attention. Approximately one month later there was a decrease in responsiveness from Bob – it seemed he was becoming quite depressed.

Tendon Release

Bob was to have an assessment on the tendons being released in his knees and ankles at the specialist hospital. The appointment was for 2pm. My Dad drove me down to Sydney as I was very nervous and concerned about him having more operations, and I didn't completely understand what the tendon releases really were. We were to meet Bob who was coming by ambulance to the hospital.

We arrived a bit early for the appointment, checked in with the receptionist and sat waiting for Bob to arrive. After about 15 minutes, I began to worry, so I asked the receptionist if she had received any updates. To my surprise, she informed me that Bob had arrived before the scheduled time and was already with the surgeon.

I knocked on the door and entered straightaway, only to find Bob in a terrible state, looking visibly scared. The doctor was recording his assessment into his dictaphone mentioning, "I've got to cut behind both left and right knees and both ankles..." However, he was not explaining the procedure or what it would entail to Bob, nor was he discussing how it would reduce pain and bring much more comfort. When I asked if he had spoken with Bob, his response was, "I didn't feel I needed to explain anything as I didn't think he would understand what I was saying".

I was so upset, feeling sick, angry and frustrated, and incredibly sad for him. So, I decided to get another opinion, only to be told that he desperately needed to have his knees done, and that the original doctor was considered the best, much to my disappointment. It was a shame about his bedside manner. I just wished they had waited for us to go in with him; after all, we were there before our appointment time. The receptionist should have informed us that he was already in with the surgeon.

It's likely very challenging for the doctors as well, as they deal with highly stressed, emotional people who haven't got a clue what decisions to make or which direction to take. However, showing compassion and understanding should indeed be part of the job.

Some surgeons had doubts about whether he could handle the anaesthetic, and we were never quite certain if he would make it through all these operations. However, it was imperative that his knees be operated on for him to achieve a much higher level of comfort. It's incredibly difficult to know what to do in such situations, especially for someone like me who lacks experience in making these decisions. I can only rely on the advice of the doctors.

In September 1989, Bob underwent a series of seven surgeries to release tendons. These procedures included releasing the tendons in both hamstrings and both Achilles tendons, as well as releasing the muscles in his left hip and groin area. Additionally, they had to divide the musculocutaneous nerve in his left arm. Because Bob's body was very delicate, they couldn't use much anaesthesia during the operations. It's difficult to imagine the pain he must have endured, and I hope I never have to experience it.

After the surgeries, Bob had to keep the bandages on for 10 days unless there was any bleeding. He was given Panadol and a small amount of pethidine to manage the pain. Fortunately, it seemed like Bob had a high tolerance for pain.

After the procedure he gained some movement in his right hand, enough to communicate with a thumbs up for yes and down for no.

I was still trying to keep the kids' lives as stable as possible; we only told them what we thought they needed to know. We kept them busy with sports activities and time with their friends was crucial. It was heartbreaking to see them unsure about what challenges we might face next. I was constantly stressed and emotionally drained; life never seemed to get easier. I was totally out of my comfort zone. Relying on the advice from the doctors and my instincts, I felt like a mess inside. Each morning, I put on a brave face as I sent the kids off to school, but afterward, I often found myself falling apart, unsure of what the day would bring.

My sister Liz and brother-in-law Max were incredibly supportive. They never questioned my decisions and stood by me through every choice I made. They would massage my stressed neck and shoulders, and whenever we found a few spare moments, we would walk on the beach to help clear my mind and sort through the decisions I had to make. I hated letting the kids see me in such a state, but this was my reality for the time being - the unpredictability of each day.

Bob's cousin, Greg, had a surprise visit from Melbourne, and the look on Bob's face was priceless, he recognised him and was so pleased to see him. Greg reminisced about shearing and running riot in their younger days - I'm kind of glad I didn't know him then, the stories were a bit too wild for me. That visit meant so much to Bob.

The Engineers and Physios were working on a special design wheelchair to make him more comfortable. This was not an easy task. Improvements in seating posture in the wheelchair were so beneficial. They started with just a normal wheelchair which I had to pay $895 for, then pulled it apart and added padded gel seating cushions, supports for hips, back and shoulders, headrests, foot plates, and armrests. This seemed to take forever and when they were happy with the chair, they asked me to pay over $14,000 for it!

I didn't exactly have that kind of money just lying around. I mentioned that I could have bought him a car for less. I wasn't familiar with the costs of wheelchairs, however that was a significant amount of money back in 1989. I knew disability needs could be costly, but I was shocked when I heard the price of that chair.

Fortunately, the hospital covered the cost of the wheelchair until the court case was held and they were reimbursed.

What a difference this chair made to his life. It was worth every penny. He could sit for hours looking very comfortable, lay right back for a snooze, or sit up and watch TV, play games, and even be taken out for a walk. He seemed so much more relaxed and comfortable.

The next mission was to get some money released from the insurance company to help pay for these types of luxuries or necessities that he needed. That became another battle, as the two insurance companies involved were still arguing over the accident and still would not accept responsibility, knowing this case was quite a big one, and hoping Bob would die before it went to court. His comfort was starting to become a real issue for him, and we had a fight on our hands with solicitors and insurance companies.

The insurance companies would send doctors down from Queensland to assess Bob and return saying he was in a vegetated state and just needed to be kept comfortable. This sounded reasonable at the time, but they didn't know the fight this man had inside him. I would sit in on some of these assessments, however I was not allowed to comment. They would ask him all kinds of questions and due to Bob's limited communication, the questions had to be yes or no answers only. They usually arrived when he was tired, so they would not get much of a response.

Living on the Central Coast

Liz and I were advised to start looking for a Nursing Home and I imagined Bob would be placed up on the Central Coast close to us. Boy was I mistaken. The National Health Scheme (NHS) was to accept Bob, however only in the nursing home that was beside the Rehabilitation Hospital in Sydney. They said he needed skilled nursing care, which he did, and they were trying to keep younger acquired brain injured patients all together in one complex. He was now 45. I had written several letters explaining we needed him closer to us here on the Central Coast, but to no avail. We were always denied our request.

I heard about a lady, Michelle, who ran her own nursing service so thought I'd try to get some advice from her. She was only too happy to help. After assessing Bob, she said he had good yes/no responses with his right thumb. She also felt he was trying to talk. He was very aware of his surroundings but trapped in that crippled body.

It was incredibly important for both me and the kids to have Bob up here on the Coast, yet our requests were consistently denied every time we applied. Michelle was an absolute angel! She assisted in writing numerous letters and made several phone calls. By knowing the correct channels to navigate, we finally managed to speak to the person in charge of approving our request. I certainly understand why they want to keep young individuals with acquired brain injuries out of aged care nursing homes, although I believed we could provide much more support if I could get him placed close to home.

Driving on the freeway from the Central Coast to Sydney was incredibly stressful, especially during rainy weather when it became very dangerous. Our time was limited; we would leave after the kids went to school and aimed to be back home before they returned. Many times, we would set out on our journey only to be forced to turn around due to accidents or severe storms on the freeway. I felt that we were putting our lives at risk by visiting him under such circumstances. Driving on the F3 (now M1) three times a week, especially when already stressed, was an ordeal, and we had to carefully choose our times to avoid peak-hour traffic. Thankfully Max, my brother-in-law, was home from work in the early afternoon most days and could look after the kids if we got held up by doctors or traffic.

I'm not sure how my beautiful sister and her husband coped with all my dramas, they were my strength, support and sanity. I'd moved in with Liz and Max and two of their three teenage boys, so with myself and my two kids, it was a very cosy household. They were amazing and I could never thank them enough. You could never prepare yourself for what we were living, and probably just as well, it would be too overwhelming.

One day we were a happy, busy, chaotic family. Suddenly, everything we thought was important in life was insignificant, our priorities changed. There were no more fun moments or laughter, and friends struggled with what to say to us. I was spending every minute in hospitals and making decisions about Bob's life, hoping desperately that they were the right ones.

We had a good marriage, but there was no time to adjust; he was suddenly ripped away from us, with no opportunity to say those special words. All at once, everything stopped; money, security, companionship, love, affection, laughter, hugs - all those things we took for granted. Our kids are grieving, unable to understand what the hell is going on. How do you comfort them and take their pain away?

On birthdays they would ask if daddy was coming home. I tried my best to find words to ease their pain, to reassure them that we're doing everything we can. But sometimes, there are no words that can fully comfort them. There were moments when I wondered if it might have been easier for us all if he had passed away on that dreadful day. At least then, we could've grieved and begun to heal. But that didn't happen, and we were left grappling with the ongoing challenges and uncertainties.

I often found myself wondering how long he could endure this existence with his twisted body, enduring constant pain, undergoing numerous operations, and facing organs that seemed to be shutting down. Yet, despite it all, he persisted with a remarkable will to live. It was both awe inspiring and heart-rending to witness.

Giru Trip - Great Friends

In the September 1989 school holidays, aware that the kids were really missing all their friends from Giru, I booked a trip back on the Greyhound bus from Doyalson to Townsville. It had been 17 months since Bob's accident. The journey stretched approximately 2,500km, long before freeways came into the picture. The bus wound its way through every tiny coastal town, pulling in to pick up and drop off fellow travellers along the way.

Dan was 11 years old and Sharna was 9. Back then, there were no iPads or mobile phones, although we did have a TV on the bus. I still remember the movie playing during the trip - Jaws. Poor Sharna was terrified and kept her head on my lap throughout the movie. Looking back, I must have been crazy to embark on a 36-hour bus trip with them. It was quite a mission for those two kids, but they were so excited.

During the journey, we played games like eye spy, spotto, coloured in, and talked. We eagerly anticipated the stops, where we could get off and stretch our legs. These days, I would dread going through such a long bus journey again.

The bus arrived in Giru at 5am, and to our surprise, nine of our friends were there to meet us. It was an incredible moment filled with tears, hugs, kids chatting excitedly all at once, laughter and smiles. Not being a morning person and totally exhausted, I was feeling very overwhelmed.

We spent two weeks there, which was a blast for the kids. They enjoyed swimming, fishing, skating, and even revisiting their old school. It was their time to have fun. Their young lives had been filled with so many challenges and adjustments, and there was still so much uncertainty ahead. But for those two weeks, it was a relief not to have any doctor's appointments or sadness surrounding us. It was a much-needed break from the everyday struggles.

Even our dog Boof, whom we had to leave behind when we moved south, was there and remembered us. There were so many questions from our dear friends, but we had few answers to give them. Tears flowed as we shared the difficulty of being apart. Despite the distance, we've remained friends with many of them to this day.

Everyone was incredibly kind and generous during those two weeks, and time seemed to fly by.

Before we knew it, we were back on the bus heading south. It was tough getting both of the kids back on board, but this time we made a stop in Brisbane to see my sister Glenys and her family, breaking up the long, tiring journey. We were relieved to finally get off that bus and sleep in a proper bed. The holiday was incredibly beneficial for all of us and much needed. Seeing the kids with their friends, laughing and being happy for a short time, was heartwarming, but it was also exhausting for me.

Pressure

Upon returning from our two-week trip, there was a lot happening with Bob, and urgent decisions needed to be made. During Bob's time in the Rehabilitation Hospital, it was noted that his general level of consciousness and awareness of his surroundings had improved throughout his admission. Despite his severe spastic quadriparesis and anarthria, he demonstrated an awareness of his environment and was able to interact in a limited manner. Although he was unable to vocalise (anarthria), his ability to comprehend and respond to simple instructions had improved. He now had a reliable yes/no response using either an eye blink or finger or foot movement.

Great improvement in his seating posture had been achieved over the last few months. By now he had undergone tenotomies of both hamstrings and both tendo-achilles, and release of the left hip adductors, musculocutaneous nerve in the left arm to significantly reduce the tight left elbow and wrist flexion contractures.

Our time was running out and we were getting pressured to where Bob might go. We were still adamant Bob needed to be up on the Central Coast, for both his well-being and ours. However, so far, there were no available beds. It seemed like he may be staying in Sydney, much to my horror. Despite applying to multiple homes, we encountered various obstacles: either there were no available beds, the cost of his feeding would be too high, or the facilities were not experienced in caring for someone with his condition. And these were just a few of the excuses we faced.

Then came the phone call we had been eagerly awaiting. After numerous discussions, questions, and negotiations, we finally received the news we had been hoping for: the green light for Bob to move up the coast. It was an immense relief for all of us, especially me and the kids.

A heartfelt thank you goes out to Michelle for her expertise and patience throughout the process. The decision marked a significant step forward for us. With Bob now just a 30-minute drive away, we could keep a closer eye on him and visit regularly.

Nursing Home

Bob's room wasn't ready when he arrived in June 1990, as it was such a rush to get him there. Our time had run out at the Rehabilitation Hospital, and they needed his bed. The staff had been incredibly supportive, teaching us how to care for Bob's special needs and arranging his wheelchair.

Everyone was so welcoming at the Nursing Home. Bob ended up with a lovely single room with his own bathroom and toilet, not that he could use it on his own. He was totally dependent on the nurses. A typical day for Bob started with getting out of bed. Before lifters were available, it would take at least two nurses to do this. He was lifted onto a commode wheelchair, strapped in and taken to the toilet where he was left until the job was done. He was then placed under the shower and washed, shaved and hair washed. After he was dressed, he would sit in his wheelchair until about 3 or 4 pm when he was put back to bed.

Once he was up and ready for the day, he was quite comfortable and didn't need a lot of attention from the staff. As long as they were there to help him feed himself lunch and the thickened fluids or have a chat, put on a video or lift him when he was uncomfortable. If he needed someone, he would bang on his tabletop or turn the volume on the TV up as loud as it would go. They would come running in to see what was wrong.

His room opened up onto the garden/BBQ area. The staff were excellent and excited to work with this delightful man. A younger resident for them who was so disabled, but still had the sense of humour from before his accident. Now to settle him in, find new doctors, speech therapists, physios, what groups he could benefit from, transport. There was so much to do.

We set up a CD stereo and played his favourite music, A TV and video player (VHS) and bought The Magnificent Seven, Crocodile Dundee, The Great Escape, and lots of westerns which he enjoyed watching immensely. I organised a massage therapist to come in twice a week and he advised us and showed the nurses how to do gentle stretches on his hands, arms, legs and neck.

He was settling in nicely and seemed happy to be in his new home and lovely surroundings. Liz and I persisted with his eating and spent hours feeding him small quantities of blended meat, vegetables, thickened fluids, custard, ice cream, etc.

Although it took a long time for Bob to eat enough to survive, the nurses didn't have the time to dedicate to feeding him adequately. Liz and I would take turns trying to encourage him to eat as much as he desired. It was crucial for him to gain weight as he was still quite thin.

We had to be careful he didn't choke. When the carers came at lunch time, they would often tell me that Bob nearly choked while they were there. He was feeding himself. He would cough, gag, hold his breath and go very red in the face, then shovel more in. It was quite scary.

He seemed to enjoy what he was eating, and it must have been nice to finally have food and flavour in his mouth. We take so much for granted until it's taken away from us. He was even starting to put on some weight now. It was nice seeing him more at ease. The tube in his stomach had to stay until he started eating more by mouth. But it caused problems like acid burns around where it went into his stomach. Changing it regularly hurt a lot, and it always looked red and painful.

We wrote the alphabet on some paper and were amazed when the right pointing finger spelt out "I love you". It took a long time to do with jagged movements, so we mounted a laminated alphabet sheet on a raised board and he could communicate at last. It was slow and he made a lot of mistakes, but it was exciting. What a wonderful feeling he was now able to communicate with words, not just yes and no answers. Where could we go from here?

Technical Aides to the Disabled were approached to construct a mechanical device, similar to the alphabet board we created, to provide greater communicative independence as well as the opportunity to maintain eye contact while communicating. After trialing 3-4 different devices, which none were successful, we found one at the Spastic Centre which he seemed to handle after a few adjustments.

It was called the Real Voice, a keyboard that printed and spoke out messages that he typed. But because his movement was so limited and jerky, the words were like a jumbled mess. They found a plastic shield to go over each letter so he had to poke his finger onto the letter he wanted to write. That worked a lot better, but it was still slow, there were lots of spelling mistakes and quite often you couldn't understand what the message was, however over time and practice he got better, and so much quicker.

Here are some of the messages that Bob would spell out:

> "My name is Ratbag Bob! This machine keeps telling me that."

"My father used to call me Bobette, cause my penis was so small he never knew if I was a boy or a girl."

"I had a dream last night that an angel came. Now my dream just came true."

"If Dan turns out like me, shoot him."

"Annie is a good sort. I don't know what she sees in me, she must love me, and I hope I can love her as much as she loves me."

"Sharna will be a nun when she grows up!" (Only someone forgot to tell Sharna that).

A summary from the speech Pathologist after setting up his communication board:

"Since the introduction of a communication device which has coincided with physical improvement, Bob has shown a great step-up in morale and now frequently smiles and laughs and loves the occasional "dirty" joke. He is a delightful man to work with and all staff and friends should be encouraged to communicate with him as frequently as possible."

There were days when we visited and got no response or he would sleep the whole time, or there was just a blank stare but slowly we could see slight improvements. He got quicker communicating with the finger movement as the right arm built up muscle tone from his newfound way to communicate.

One day I asked him if he knew who I was. I wasn't prepared for his answer.

He went through all of his old girlfriends, Bernadette, Carmel, Mary, etc. and then his sister. When I said, "No, I'm not any of them", he spelt "Does it really matter?"

Yes, you bet it did, because none of them were there or came to visit him. I was pretty pissed off, and as I bent down to pick up my bag he spelt out "you are Annie".

The one thing that didn't seem to change was his sense of humour and personality. I thought, "Asshole". I was so angry, confused and stressed. I couldn't see the funny side of his answer then, as I can now.

We joined a Community Access group for people with an acquired Brain Injury and I was getting a lot of support from the people involved. Many were young men that had motor vehicle accidents, like Bob. One had been in a public phone box, ringing his parents to come and pick him up when a drunk driver lost control and slammed into it. Witnessing these young men in such situations was heartbreaking. Most of them were even younger than Bob, and their parents, presuming they were beyond the need for parental care, were often elderly and appeared exhausted.

With brain injuries no two are the same. Some become angry, frustrated, aggressive, confused and unresponsive. We were lucky with Bob as his personality stayed much the same. He never seemed to complain unless he was uncomfortable or in a lot of pain.

News Story

I woke up one morning and gazed into the mirror and didn't recognise the reflection staring back at me. I had aged. I looked worn out and I was not even 40 yet. That moment was a wake-up call - I knew I needed to make changes in my life. Despite the weight of caring for Bob and making crucial decisions, I also had to consider the well-being of my two young children. If I fell apart, what would happen to them?

Financially, times were tough. Despite receiving a small pension, I had to stretch it to cover expenses for Bob. Money was tight, with only $30 left each fortnight and no room for extras. Determined to improve my situation, I enrolled in a bar course, thinking I could work at night while Liz and Max looked after the kids, but that was not for me.

Instead, I embarked on a job hunt, going from shop to shop and leaving my name (resumes weren't common back then). With a background in retail, I knew the industry well. My break came when I landed a few days of work at a local pharmacy. It wasn't much at first, but it was a start. Even as I worked, visiting Bob three times a week felt like a full-time job in itself. Between doctor's appointments, legal matters, and hospital visits, there was always something demanding my attention.

I worked in a pharmacy until the day I retired.

The local paper had caught wind of our situation and expressed interest in writing a story about a young man in a nursing home.

Initially, I wasn't keen on the idea, but The CASS Group thought it could be beneficial for our cause, so I reluctantly agreed. I met with the reporter, who arranged a meeting with Bob, the kids, and myself at the nursing home.

The meeting went smoothly, but when the article appeared in the paper the following week, I was shocked and distraught. While there was a lovely photo of Bob and I on page 4, all the information provided was wrong. When I contacted the reporter, she confessed that she had lost our interview and had to rely on memory to piece together the story. Unfortunately, she got it completely wrong, even misquoting me as saying "people were telling me to walk away, move on with your life." Furthermore, the kids' names were incorrect. I was furious!

The next week, there was an apology for the misinformation in our story, but it was little consolation. It felt like an unnecessary ordeal, and I couldn't help but wonder why I had bothered to do the interview in the first place.

Community Access & Support Service (CASS)

Bob had settled into life at the Nursing Home quite well. However, as time went on, we noticed that Bob was becoming bored and depressed. The activities available at the Nursing Home, such as Bingo and occasional concerts, were not enough to stimulate him. With eighty other residents and only one activities officer, the staff were stretched thin, and rehabilitation was not a focus in their training. Bob often found himself spending a lot of time alone, as the staff were busy and, although kind, were limited by time and understaffing.

Recognising the need for more stimulation, we organised for carers to come to the Nursing Home. We knew that despite the challenges, we were fortunate that the nursing home had accepted Bob, especially after the fight to bring him up to the Coast. However, we also knew that addressing this issue would be crucial for his well-being.

CASS, a support service for people with acquired brain injuries and their families, was exactly what he needed.

After meeting Bob, CASS organised carers to come 2-3 times a week. They would take him out for walks, through the gardens, or down to the lake, play scrabble, or word games. James was a favourite; he was so caring and compassionate with him. They worked so well together, and he always left me messages of how they spent their time. Other carers, Christine, Annette, Deanne and Buck were also terrific and certainly made an improvement in the quality of his life.

He would name an animal, a town, or a boy and girl's name, starting with each letter of the alphabet. He took this very seriously and when trying to think of animals starting with N, he came up with nanny goats, which always seemed to make me laugh. He was quite well travelled and loved doing the town names. It would take ages, as he would tell you he had been to each town, or sheared sheep there.

Bob enjoyed these days immensely and took it all so seriously. His spelling was very inadequate and many times you had to try and guess what he was spelling out, like Eupulepust (Eucalyptus) or Brilnt (Brillant), but he just loved the one-on-one visits. He talked about the kids, telling James that Sharna was going to be a nun. When I say 'talked', I mean spelling out on the communication board.

We joined the local club where he went to Bingo each week, quite often winning a meat tray, chocolates, or some money. He would often try and trade the chocolate for a kiss. On a Thursday he would go Ten Pin Bowling. The ladies loved seeing him arrive and Bob always looked so eager to win. They would set a ramp up beside the alley, put the bowling ball on, and Bob would tell them what angle to turn it, then with his pointer finger on his twisted right hand he would send it down the ramp.

He got a score of 200 one day and they presented him with a bowling pin all signed by the staff. He loved it and proudly displayed it on a shelf in his room. He told me once that the pins had magnets on the bottom, which is why you can't get a strike. He always had a good excuse!

All the carers loved working with him as he entertained them with his stories. It was hard to feel sorry for him as he was so positive. If you felt down when you went to visit him, he would lift you, and you would leave with a smile. There were always issues with his communication board, not being charged, out of paper or just not working, it was an antique. When it was working, it was his escape to the outside world, to us and the people around him. He had been trapped in that body for years, so it was important it worked.

We had dedicated a lot of effort to setting up activities, care plans, and communication strategies for Bob, and we were beginning to see some benefits and slight improvements. As part of this, we installed a TV/VCR high on his wall and attempted to teach him how to use the remote control. He only needed to use the channel and volume buttons, but as anyone who has dealt with remotes knows, they can be quite confusing, and pressing the wrong button could result in a different language, a fuzzy screen, or a split screen. It wasn't difficult to accidentally mess up the programs.

To mitigate this, we covered most of the buttons, improvising with a soap container that could cover the unnecessary buttons. It was firm enough to provide protection but not too hard so Bob could still grip it, and if dropped, it wouldn't break. Despite the challenges, Bob's learning process with the remote control was ongoing, with the remote often disappearing, ending up in the wash, or getting lost in his bed.

However, we were slowly making progress and getting results. As long as the nurses positioned him in front of the TV, he could see it and enjoy his entertainment. Bob certainly kept us on our toes and gave us plenty to think about.

We discovered that Bob had a fondness for watching movies, and he had his favourites. Films like Crocodile Dundee, The Great Escape, The Magnificent Seven, The Man from Snowy River, and They're a Weird Mob were among his top picks. He would become fixated on one movie and watch it repeatedly for weeks on end, often forgetting that he had seen it before. However, it didn't matter to him; he was content watching it over and over again.

I lost count of how many times I had to buy the same VHS tape because they would wear out from frequent use. It was a relief when DVDs were invented, saving us from constantly replacing worn-out tapes. Back then, there was no Netflix or YouTube, and oh, how convenient they would have been!

Weekly Visits

Every Wednesday after getting the kids off to school, Liz and I would pack a picnic lunch and spend the day at the Nursing Home, which was about a 30-minute drive. Bob loved this day and never stopped spelling out messages. We would arrive at about 10am. Sometimes he would still be in bed, other times he was up and waiting and looked really good. We never quite knew what we were about to find when we walked into his room.

His feet were always like ice so we would rub them, put woollen socks and lambswool slippers on. We would clean his wheelchair which always had food all over it from the fluids that went into his peg site. His communication machine always needed cleaning, as it would also get food caked over it, or it needed charging and the paper roll renewed.

When the weather was nice we would take him out into the garden or go for a walk. We talked about old friends, growing up, what he did for work, holidays, the kids. He was often known as Bullshit Bob, Ratbag Bob or Have a Chat (short for 'Nit Nat Have a Chat Beer Bottle Bob'), which suited him perfectly.

As Liz and I walked in the door, he would spell out,

"I had a dream that an angel would come to visit me, and my dream just came true". Such a lovely welcome.

I always made sure to take a That's Life magazine down for Bob, knowing he enjoyed doing the puzzles or 'use his brain', as he would tell us. His favourites were Find the Words and Arrow Words. Each week, after he completed the puzzles, I would send them into the magazine in the hopes of winning some prizes. He actually won $50 once or twice, and he would get so excited, urging Liz and I to go shopping and buy ourselves a new hat. We couldn't help but laugh, knowing that neither of us really suited hats very well.

He loved playing Scrabble and he would try to look at our tiles and help make our words. We were playing one day and nearly finished the game when he sneezed, his knee flew up, hit the tray table and the tiles all went flying through the air. We just stared in amazement and laughed.

Bob had a remarkable way of lifting your spirits whenever you were feeling down, stressed, exhausted, or just flat. He never complained or expressed anger, just genuinely happy to have a visitor. We made it a point to be there for lunch each visit, and it brought him such joy.

Fortunately, he was eating quite well by mouth now, using a special bent spoon to feed himself, and he really savoured his food. Despite still having the peg feed in his stomach, which caused him discomfort, he found great pleasure in indulging in treats like Milo ice cream or mousse, as well as blended paw-paw or fruit. His eyes would light up with excitement whenever we brought down those little Furry Friends chocolates, as he had a particular fondness for chocolate.

We stretched and massaged his arms, neck, shoulders and legs, he must have been in horrific pain, but still never complained. We'd lather the QV cream on his face.

He liked to have a moustache which I had to trim and shape. He would bless himself because I had scissors near his face. It must have been terrifying watching me shaking while cutting it. He would try to spell out messages while I was doing it so we had to take his board away, then he would pretend to get angry.

His fingernails were always so long and hard digging into his soft flesh on the palms of his hands. The fingers were all bent and contorted, you had to be a contortionist to get to them. We certainly earned our money. Oh, hang on, we didn't get paid for these visits. Guess you call it a love job.

He was only on Panadol for the pain, but thankfully with the severe brain damage he didn't seem to feel a lot of pain.

When Princess Diana died, he cried and was so emotional, he was in quite a state. It was the first time we had seen that emotional side. The next day I asked if he knew who the important person was who had died, and he told me The Prime Minister. He had forgotten. When I told him it was Princess Diana, he cried again.

Dan, Sharna and I would visit most Saturdays, he was always so pleased to see them and wanted to know how they were doing at school, what sports they were playing, who their mates were, and so on. Dan found it extremely hard, he just wanted his dad back, just to hear his voice, have a father-son chat, go fishing or play soccer with him. He didn't tell many people what had happened to his dad, and kept it very close to his heart. I felt so sad for him, but he wouldn't let me or anyone in.

Sharna seemed to cope differently and could tell him what she was doing, playing netball, nippers and hanging out with her friends. But as long as I was around she seemed to cope.

It was hard for them to sacrifice their Saturdays. We never knew how Bob would respond when we arrived. Some days there was no response where he just slept the whole visit, or he had soiled himself. Other days he would spell out messages and be so happy to see them. He would always keep us there for as long as possible spelling out just one more message, but would finish with: "Drive safely and keep an eye out for all the drunks".

His sister Roslyn, who lived in Victoria on a cattle property, came to visit a couple of times a year. Seeing her brother in such a state was extremely difficult for her. I attempted to prepare her and explain that despite his condition, he seemed content, but it remained challenging for her to witness.

Bob and Roslyn had been fostered at the ages of 2 and 3 and had a very different childhood to most kids. Bob left the family around the age of 17, travelling Australia and New Zealand, shearing sheep and working in the mines, while Roslyn stayed on the farm. They hadn't been in contact for quite a few years when I met Bob.

Understanding the importance of family ties, I suggested that Bob reconnect with them, as they were the only family he knew. We eventually made a trip to Victoria to meet them. At the time, Dan was about 18 months old, allowing Bob the opportunity to introduce Dan to his father, Jim. Sadly, Bob's mother had passed away a few years earlier.

I remember the day when I placed a pen in his hand while Roslyn was visiting, and instantly he wrote, "I love you," without hesitation, so proud of himself, laughing and giving the thumbs up. Now he could write, although very shaky and slow. There were lots of tears when we witnessed it. He never ceased to amaze us all. He could now write on birthday cards for Dan and Sharna, although it took up the whole card.

Starting Again

My life had become so wrapped up in Bob's that my body was struggling. I was experienced headaches, mouth ulcers, and soreness everywhere I touched. I booked myself in for a few massages, which really seemed to help, but I needed something just for me.

The kids had settled into sports and had each made new friends, so in my spare time (if you can call it that!), I found a tennis competition nearby. I had always been very sporty and gave 100% in any game I played. Realising I had a lot of frustration to release, this was just what I needed. It was a mixed group; some were just there for a laugh, but I certainly wasn't.

This is where I met Phil, who also enjoyed a challenge. He was a builder, a surfer, and a keen golfer, and he still is to this day. He lived alone with his faithful blue heeler dog, Pepper. He had no idea about my story and showed no pity for me on the court. When we realised he lived only a couple of streets from me, we decided to take turns driving to tennis each week.

Then he asked me out for dinner. Not having been on a date for a long, long time and feeling as I did, I was very nervous. But then I thought about how nice it might be.

We chatted easily and were having a lovely time, then he asked me about my situation. Assuming I was separated or divorced, I hesitated. I didn't really want to reveal my circumstances, thinking, "You don't want to know what I am going through." I could only imagine his response.

After a long internal debate, I finally responded:

"I am not separated or divorced. My husband of 13 years was a passenger in the company ute on his way to work. The driver, blinded by the sun, turned in front of a fully loaded semi-trailer. The driver was killed, and Bob is now a quadriplegic with severe brain damage. I have to make every decision in his life, I have two small children, and I live with my sister and her family. My life is hell, and I have so much baggage."

The look on the poor guy's face was one of utter shock and disbelief. I thought he might excuse himself to the toilet and do a runner, but he didn't. Instead, he said, "You always look so happy and smiling?" We laugh about it now, but back then, it was so raw. As he got to know me, he discovered that I didn't always smile - I cried a lot as well.

We're still together over 30 years later, a blended family of 5 children and 13 grandchildren. It hasn't been an easy journey by any means, although it has been very interesting.

Phil and I even built our open-plan house all on one level so we could bring Bob home on special occasions - Father's Day, birthdays, Christmas, and so on, which he loved.

Celebrating our first Christmas together with Phil and his three kids, Brett, Craig and Carley, we were at Liz and Max's house when the disabled taxi arrived with Bob. He was wearing a Santa hat, had presents for the kids, and looked very smart. There was a large crowd, and people were all going up and chatting with him.

He was spelling out messages and was very excited about being with the family. While Liz and I were getting lunch ready, Phil thought he would have a chat with him. They had met a couple of times by now. You never knew what he would say or what he knew, so when he spelt out to poor Phil, "Do you want me to die?" and then looked at him with a very serious face, Phil thought, "He knows I am with his wife now!"

Phil said, "No, Bob, why would you say that?" and Bob replied, "Well then, give me something to eat, otherwise I'll starve to death." There was a relieved look on many faces, especially Phil's.

We had explained Phil to Bob, and he seemed content enough that I was seeing someone, but you never knew what was going on in his head. On one occasion, while we were visiting him, he pointed to me and spelt, "I've been wondering which one of us is best in bed," then he laughed. I nearly fell off the chair, and there they were, both looking at me with strange faces.

We purchased a bus with a wheelchair lifter from a retirement village with the intention of converting it into a motorhome. Sometimes on weekends, we would collect Liz and Max, then pick up Bob from the Nursing Home and have a picnic lunch and a drive around the coast. Bob loved these outings, often pointing at Phil who was driving. He would bless himself and tell Phil he was going over too many bumps, or he was a mug driver. There was never a dull moment.

We live in such a beautiful area, a strip of land with lakes on one side and the beach on the other. There are plenty of places to explore and drive around.

Camp Breakaway

Camp Breakaway was a registered non-profit charitable organisation that specialised in providing people with disabilities and their carers a holiday experience. Bob had the privilege of attending three of these wonderful camps. I must admit, I was initially nervous when I saw the activities program, as I didn't think he would be able to participate in many of them.

However, I couldn't have been more wrong. The week was packed with entertainment, including activities like motorcycle and sidecar rides, sailing, mini-Olympics, bowling, fishing, and visits to the reptile park. Each camper had their own carer, and there were trained medical staff on hand to ensure everyone's safety.

The Harley Davidsons arrived, and seeing the excited look on Bob's face as they slid his twisted body into the sidecar was truly heartwarming. He always had his own motorbike and loved them, and he always dreamed of owning a Harley Davidson. This was like a dream come true for him.

Our joy quickly turned to concern when Bob suddenly looked distressed and upset. Thankfully, the biker brought him back, and after providing him with the communication board, Bob spelled out, "You need gloves on if you are going to ride a Harley." We were all so relieved, and we immediately tried to put gloves on his bent and twisted hands. Bob's infectious smile soon returned, and we were all able to enjoy the experience together.

The next day, buses took the campers to the Belmont 16ft Sailing Club, where all the little yachts awaited the competitors. Sailability, a nationwide organisation dedicated to facilitating sailing for everyone, regardless of age and disability, had organised the event. Bob was incredibly enthusiastic, looking as though he was embarking on a journey to New Zealand rather than just a sailing competition. He gave a big thumbs up and laughed as he went past, clearly enjoying the excitement of the moment.

Bob Turner was always a hit with his Wildlife Show at Camp Breakaway. He would often put a snake around Bob's neck or bring a crocodile near him for him to touch, much to Bob's delight. Witnessing Bob's joy was incredibly precious for all of us. The looks of sheer wonder on the faces of the other campers said it all.

The week concluded with a beautiful candlelight dinner and concert. Everything was provided for us, from beds and linen to food and transportation, along with a week filled with amazing entertainment. By the end of the week, Bob was exhausted, but he had enjoyed every single minute and couldn't wait for the next camp to come around.

The demand for spots at Camp Breakaway was so high that we could only manage to get Bob there every 2nd or 3rd year. Despite the limited frequency, the experience was always incredible. Camp Breakaway is truly a wonderful organisation.

What struck me most about the camp was the dedication of the staff, all of whom were volunteers. It was clear that they were genuinely committed to creating a memorable experience for the campers. My sister Liz has dedicated over 30 years to volunteering as a carer. Her countless contributions have earned her life membership in the organisation. Now, at the vibrant young age of 79, she's still actively volunteering and making a difference. These camps offer a truly rewarding experience for both the campers and the volunteers alike.

Bob summed it up perfectly with his comment, "If you want to get free from your disabilities and worries, come to Camp Breakaway. The holiday was great." His words speak volumes about the impact of Camp Breakaway on those who attend.

Solicitors

I had to engage solicitors in Townsville and also find someone to work for Bob on the Central Coast. I was instructed to keep all his receipts, so I bought a book and meticulously recorded every expense. It was astonishing how quickly it all added up, and yet there was still no assistance from the insurers. We maintained a detailed record of all costs, including petrol, wear and tear on my car, clothing, skincare, haircuts, lambswool for his bed and wheelchair, postage, tolls on freeways, pharmacy expenses, communication, TV, radio, cassettes, and more.

I made special bibs for him as his shirts were constantly soaked due to dribbling. These bibs went over his shoulders with a collar and resembled shirts rather than traditional bibs. They had a plastic lining to prevent his chest from getting wet, making them look much nicer than simple terry towelling bibs. I had to buy him size 12 children's clothes because of the significant weight loss he experienced. He was down to 48 kilograms.

Due to his brain injury, his skin was dry, flaky, and red. Using soap only exacerbated the issue, so after trying various skincare ranges, we found that EGO QV or Dermaveen worked best for him. The skin on his face would often build up into crusty, weeping sores, so the staff needed to be vigilant with washing his face.

During winter, his feet would become like ice due to poor circulation, so we had a lady knit special wool socks for him. They were bright red, but they looked incredibly warm, so we didn't worry about the colour.

The doctors mentioned that my visits had a therapeutic effect on Bob, so they suggested I should be reimbursed for my travel costs. During my visits, I would massage his legs, arms, neck, and hands, and perform gentle stretches. Cutting his nails was no easy task, as his fingers were all twisted and bent back. I also made sure to be there when his lunch arrived. Although he was learning to feed himself with specially designed utensils, it was a slow and messy process at first. However, he improved as he started to enjoy more food and gained more movement in his arms.

To claim reimbursement, I had to provide the number of kilometres I travelled each week to visit him. They allowed me $0.35 per kilometre, which sounded great, but I had to pay for everything upfront. I visited him three times a week, spending five hours each visit. The round trip from home to the nursing home was 60 kilometres. I was immensely grateful to have him on the Coast instead of in Sydney.

The solicitors in QLD were rather negligent, failing to answer or return my phone calls or messages. It seemed too challenging for them now that we had moved interstate, and the file had been moved to the "too hard" basket. We had been attempting to secure funds for a new wheelchair, but they would not respond to any of my attempts to contact them. I was becoming increasingly frustrated with the lack of response, and my solicitors on the Coast shared the sentiment.

Feeling that this case was too complex for my current solicitors, I made the decision to explore other options, including a Compensation Company. Someone had recommended some Compensation Lawyers, so after a phone call, I decided to schedule our first meeting.

On the 4th of April 1995, myself, Liz, Max, and my dad travelled to Sydney for our meeting. The lawyer was very friendly, welcoming, and apologetic for the way the system had failed so miserably with our case. He made it clear that this case was never going to be an easy one. Liability would not be a problem; the only issue was quantum, that is, how much compensation. However, this is a significant case, and we can expect the insurance companies to vigorously oppose it. For that reason, it needs to be vigorously fought on our side. It's unfortunate that the case is in Queensland, as ideally, he would prefer to have it heard in New South Wales. It could be expedited more quickly and at a lower cost.

We left the meeting feeling confused, stressed, but also more confident, albeit with a huge decision to make. It meant we would also have to cover the other solicitors' out-of-pocket expenses for the work they had already undertaken, which could amount to about $20,000, and hopefully reach an agreement regarding their professional fees at the end. If the case couldn't be moved to NSW, then we would have to work through a QLD solicitor, which was less than ideal but perhaps unavoidable.

It felt like I was back at square one, but he assured me that I would have two specialist teams working together. There was a lot to think about. He also mentioned that after 7 long years, we were looking at least another 7 given the current pace of proceedings. There was an immense amount of work ahead of us.

On the 1st of August 1995, 7 years after the accident, I finally gave the go-ahead to the Compensation Lawyers to take over the case. The scary thing was that I had to sign a fee agreement, and as I had never been involved with any solicitors before, this was way out of my league - I was terrified.

Suddenly, things were starting to move. The lawyer had written to both solicitors and received the files. Workers Comp, Social Security, Medicare, the Taxation Office, hospitals, out-of-pocket expenses - the list went on and on, and all this money paid out had to be repaid. Little did I know what was still ahead of me.

Court

After ten long years, our court case finally had a date set for May 1998. I'm convinced the insurers dragged it out, hoping Bob would pass away before they had to pay a claim. In March, the insurance company offered a settlement, but it was an insult. It would hardly cover the costs up to date, let alone future care.

I was informed that our case would be heard in Townsville, and my solicitors believed it would be advantageous to bring Bob along. Initially, I was against it, wondering how on earth we would manage such a trip. Organising travel for someone in Bob's condition would be a full-time job and come with its fair share of headaches. However, my solicitors outlined my responsibilities:

1. Find accommodation in Townsville for Bob.

2. Compile a list of all his disability needs, including a bed, shower chairs, feeding poles, and food - it was a daunting list.

3. Secure a nurse to accompany him on the trip and during his stay in Townsville, although the duration was uncertain.

4. Arrange a nursing company in Townsville.

5. Coordinate transportation to Sydney airport via a disabled taxi.

6. Organise a disabled taxi upon arrival.

7. Arrange transportation and accommodation for Liz and myself.

It might not sound like much, but I was working four days a week, visiting Bob whenever possible, supporting my family, and trying to cope with everything. Needless to say, I was incredibly stressed. My boss, Richard, was incredibly understanding and supportive. He didn't add to the stress, even with the numerous phone calls I received during work hours. I'm immensely grateful to him.

Securing accommodation proved to be a significant challenge. Who would be willing to accommodate a quadriplegic with severe brain damage? I contacted every nursing home, hospital, care accommodation facility, and even reached out to the Red Cross, but all I received were apologies and rejections.

Then, I contacted the Sheraton Townsville Hotel & Casino, situated on the marina overlooking Townsville Harbour. To my surprise, they informed me that they had disabled rooms and would be happy to accommodate us. I explained the situation, outlining our need for a rented bed with rails, peg feeding equipment, special blended food requirements, shower chairs, toilet chairs, and a myriad of other necessities. Despite the extensive list, they responded with a resounding "Yes, we can do this."

I made it clear that there would be numerous people coming and going, but they reassured me that they were more than willing to accommodate our needs. They were incredibly understanding and accommodating, going above and beyond to assist us. It was a huge relief to cross off this daunting task from my ever-growing list.

I initially thought that arranging for a nurse to travel and care for Bob during our trip wouldn't be too difficult. However, it turned out to be quite a challenge. I considered the possibility of a staff member from Bob's nursing home accompanying us, as they were familiar with Bob's needs and were fond of him. Unfortunately, this option was not permitted by the nursing home.

After numerous phone calls to Green Nurses and various nursing services, I reached a point of frustration. I informed my solicitors that it was proving too difficult for me to arrange a nurse, and if they wanted Bob to accompany us to Townsville, they would need to find someone themselves.

To my relief, they contacted me the next day, informing me that they had successfully arranged for a male nurse to accompany Bob. It seemed that they knew the right strings to pull and were accustomed to handling such arrangements. While it was a challenge for me, I was grateful that they were able to sort it out.

I only ever used the one disabled taxi company, whose drivers were truly wonderful and patient with Bob. They were more than happy to assist us in getting to Sydney airport, making that part of the journey relatively easy.

On the day of our trip to Townsville, Liz and I met Bob and the taxi on a Saturday. We had our flight with ANSETT scheduled to depart at 12:55pm to Brisbane, then another flight at 14:20, arriving in Townsville at 16:45. It was going to be a long journey.

We had packed bags filled with special clothes for Bob, his communication board, chargers, incontinence pads, sheepskins, feeding tubes, medication, food for the trip, and special soaps and skincare products. This was all before suitcases had wheels, so it felt like we were carrying a ton of weight. And, of course, there was our own luggage to contend with as well. We felt like pack horses.

As we set off, Liz once again left her family behind, and I left my two teenagers and Phil. It was a significant departure for all of us.

Col, the taxi driver, remarked, "Bob's tyres look a little flat, so we might just put a bit of air in at this servo," as we headed towards the airport. Upon arrival, we nearly left one of Bob's bags in the taxi, only realising at the last minute that it was missing. We were supposed to meet Andrew, the nurse, at the service desk. We had no idea what he looked like, or how skilled he would be in caring for Bob, but it wouldn't be difficult for him to spot us.

As I was at the counter picking up the four tickets that my solicitor had organised for our flights, I heard an almighty bang. Turning around in alarm, not knowing what I would be faced with, I saw people crouching down. Then I noticed Bob sitting at a terrible angle and realised one of his tyres had exploded!

What a dreadful start to the trip! With everything closing in Townsville around 2pm on weekends, our options were limited. Thankfully, Robbie still lived there. I immediately called him, explaining our situation, and asked him to get tyres, tubes, and a bike pump. I provided him with all the necessary sizes and arranged to meet him at the airport. I was in a state of panic due to the situation.

As we waited for assistance, Bob remained occupied spelling out messages throughout the journey to Townsville. We had no way of knowing if he fully comprehended what was happening or where he was going. When my solicitors asked me what

I thought Bob might say when he went into court, whether he would know where he was, I could only respond, "I have no idea." After all, who knows what goes on in his head.

We finally arrived in Townsville, feeling tired and exhausted, but relieved that we had made it. Thankfully, Robbie was there with the repair kit, so we immediately set to work changing the tube and tyre in the arrival room at the airport.

With the tyre issue resolved, our next priority was to secure a disabled taxi and transport Bob to the Sheraton, where we had already arranged for a room filled with all the equipment he would need for our stay in Townsville. However, the uncertainty of how long the court case would last posed a challenge. Would it be 2 days, 3, 4, or even 5? Trying to stay organised amidst the unpredictability was proving to be quite difficult.

Andrew, the nurse accompanying us, proved to be invaluable. He took care of bathing and feeding Bob while I communicated all of his requirements to the hotel staff. We also had Green Nurses on standby to provide additional assistance.

Liz and I ended up staying with Robbie since I had forgotten to book accommodation. He even lent us his car, but there was a slight oversight - we didn't know the make or colour. When he handed me the keys, it didn't occur to either of us to ask. So, when we went to leave the Sheraton, we found ourselves at a loss, staring at each other and bursting into laughter. We were utterly exhausted.

Without mobile phones to call and ask Robbie about his car, we resorted to wandering through the car park, clicking the button on the keys and waiting for a car to beep. We must have looked like we were about to steal a car. What a day it had been, from the early morning mishap of nearly leaving Bob's bag behind in the taxi, to the tyre exploding at the airport, and Bob charming the air hostesses with his sweet talk and compliments, telling them how beautiful they were. Then there was the task of meeting new nurses for the first time and explaining Bob's needs, all while juggling his food and fluids.

It was a day we would never forget.

Sunday was a much-needed rest day for all of us, especially for Bob, who spent the day in bed. It was a welcome break before the court proceedings began. Bob's room was quite nice with a view over the marina which certainly added some relaxing vibes. However, the space was filled to the brim with all the hired equipment Bob needed.

Later that evening, our barrister and solicitors arranged to meet with Bob in his room. They asked him a series of questions, aiming to gauge his awareness. Although still fatigued from the previous day, Bob managed to impress them with his answers and enthusiastic attitude. He takes moments like this very seriously, but in truth, who knows what's truly going on in his mind.

The court case went on for 3 days, and Bob was not required to attend until the final day. Andrew would take him for walks along The Strand and the Marina. He loved looking at the boats, which no doubt would have brought back memories of his time working on the prawn trawlers out of Townsville. He enjoyed the walks and attention but mostly the fresh air and the interaction with Andrew. They were quite a pair.

Meanwhile, Liz and I were present in court every day. It was a profound experience for us, listening to the Lawyers giving their opinions, fighting from one to the other. The insurers had sent doctors to assess Bob on various occasions, believing they had accurately depicted his condition as vegetative, asserting that he simply needed comfort care. However, we knew there was more to Bob Warren than what met the eye. It was fascinating to hear their perspectives and what they believed Bob required in his life.

Little did they know what a formidable fighter Bob Warren truly was.

On the third day, Bob was scheduled to take the stand, and our anxiety levels were through the roof. We were unsure if he knew where he was and we had no idea what he might say.

His communication board was fully charged and ready for action. Bob looked very dapper in his best clothes, with his moustache neatly trimmed and what remained of his hair tidily groomed, as we wheeled him into the courtroom.

Once inside, we were not permitted to talk or sit with him, so we took our seats and anxiously observed his actions. We noticed him typing away on his board, his expression serious. I feared he might spell out a deeply personal or embarrassing anecdote, such as his father calling him 'Bobette' because his penis was so small they couldn't tell if he was a boy or girl.

Liz and I exchanged worried glances, anticipating what he might reveal. We didn't have to wait long, as soon as the judge entered the room, Bob pressed the talk button, and the message was clear:

"I would like to apologise to the judge for not standing up".

Not one spelling mistake. I, for one, was in total shock.

The look on the Insurers faces was so rewarding for us; their mouths dropped open and their eyes bulged out of their heads. It was truly priceless. Over the past decade, I've had to fight tooth and nail to secure absolutely anything we needed for him. The struggle had been relentless.

The judge accepted Bob's apology, and Bob, in response, gave him a thumbs-up. When asked about his interests in sport, Bob confidently claimed, "Yes, I once played cricket with Donald Bradman and helped train the Collingwood Footy Club." In his mind, he truly believed it to be the case.

When asked about gardening, Bob's response was…

"I always grew our vegetables. My mother said I grew the best beans that they would blow your asshole out."

The stenographer, Jenny, struggled to understand what the American voice machine was saying, so the judge asked Bob to repeat his message. That happened twice, with Jenny still unable to fully understand the message. Eventually, I was asked to come down to the courtroom to read what Bob had written. I was so embarrassed as I knew what he said. Nevertheless, I had to step forward and read aloud to the courtroom what was displayed on the screen.

When I left the asshole bit out, Bob thumped on his tabletop, and got quite angry. The Judge knew I hadn't read it right. He asked me to read it again, exactly as Bob had written it. So, I reluctantly read it completely. Jenny nodded and told the judge she got it now.

The courtroom burst into laughter and Bob was very pleased with himself. He gave the Judge the thumbs up and laughed until he started coughing and nearly fell out of his chair. It was a success taking him to court.

During the lunch break, Liz and I ventured down the street for a quick bite to eat. As we made our way back to court, we noticed a parking officer about to issue a ticket for Robbie's car, as the parking meter had just expired. Realising it wasn't our car, I called out, "No! We are coming" and started running to the car. However, in the background, a voice called out, "Don't worry Mrs. Warren, the Insurance Company will pay it." When I turned around, I saw my solicitor and barristers' team with the insurers, all having lunch together. I was stunned and feeling so naive. They all appeared as though they were mates - like playing against the opposition on a football team, only to hug each other after the match. What an eye opener for Liz and I.

The policeman who had attended the accident site was present in court that day. He recounted how they hadn't expected Bob to survive; they initially thought he had died, so they focused on extracting the driver. Unfortunately, the driver had died at the scene. When I asked the policeman if he would like to meet Bob, he agreed.

Upon explaining to Bob that this policeman had been the one to rescue him from the ute, Bob immediately typed out a message: "I would like to thank you for saving my life," and then gave the policeman a thumbs up. The policeman was brought to tears and overcome with emotion. He said they respond to accidents all the time, however it's not often they get to meet the survivors, like Bob. He was overwhelmed. It was very touching for everyone involved.

Dollar figures were thrown around, and we were faced with the decision of whether to build Bob a house so he could be cared for at home, or to continue with his care in the nursing home while having carers come in to stimulate him. Thanks to the diligent work of my barristers and solicitors, Bob was set up to have a comfortable life, no matter the decision.

After everything was settled, Liz and I found ourselves driving our barristers and solicitors to the airport in our borrowed car. It was a surreal moment as they commended us on the wonderful job we had done with Bob and expressed their pleasure in working on his case. They even gave us a kiss on the cheek before heading for the departure terminal. We sat there in shock, unable to believe what had just happened. It's a memory that still makes me laugh to this day.

What a whirlwind of emotions that day had been. So much to process. That evening, Bob and I decided to treat our special friends, who had been on this nightmare journey with us, to dinner, even though Bob couldn't eat the food. We were at the Casino Marina, so I gave Bob $20 to play the pokies. He was so excited.

We don't know if he really knew what had just happened that day or where he was, but he did so perfectly well. Understanding the complexities of Bob's brain injury was like unravelling a mystery.

The following day, as we wheeled him across the tarmac to the plane, we couldn't help but notice that his dignity comfort pants had come apart, leaving his bare bum exposed for all to see. We couldn't help but laugh at the absurdity of the situation. Here he was, now a millionaire, with his bum exposed to the world.

We knew that this money had to last him for the rest of his life. The Public Trustee was appointed to manage Bob's finances, a responsibility I was grateful to hand over. We could finally afford to purchase the things that would make Bob's life just a bit more comfortable. Although we still had to seek approval from the Public Trustee for expenditures, they were supportive, allowing me to proceed with Bob's needs.

There were numerous outstanding accounts that needed to be settled: Workers Compensation, Townsville Hospital, the Annex Hospital, the Rehabilitation Hospital, Social Security, Solicitors, the Nursing Home - the list seemed endless. The total sum amounted to over a million dollars. It's worth noting that a year prior, we were offered $1.5 million to settle, an offer I'm grateful we refused. Finally, after a decade of struggle, we could achieve closure. It was a tremendous relief and promised to make our lives considerably easier. Now, if Bob needed a new wheelchair or a masseur to tend to his muscles, or even just basic skin care products or clothing, I could arrange it. However, there were still countless decisions to be made.

Firstly, managing Bob's needs felt like a full-time job in itself, in addition to juggling the needs of our two children who had lost their father, as they knew him. Secondly, maintaining my own full-time job, which provided a welcome distraction from the constant decision-making and dramas that came with caring for Bob. Thirdly, I found myself making decisions that no one should ever have to make for someone else's life - decisions about medical procedures or whether to pursue treatment when Bob's health took a turn. Lastly, navigating a full-time relationship with a partner who was understanding and supportive was crucial. Thankfully, my partner proved to be just that, as it just wouldn't have worked if he questioned all of my decisions. His children, Brett, Craig, and Carley appeared pleased that their father had found a companion. Little did they know the full extent of my story when they first met me.

Snow Trip Holiday

After the court case, I promised Dan and Sharna a holiday, asking them where they would like to go. I expected them to suggest Fiji or Bali, but to my surprise, they both agreed on a ski trip. Sharna had enjoyed a school excursion to Canberra and the Snowy Mountains previously, so she was keen to return, but it was Dan's first-time seeing snow. I was quite surprised at their response.

We booked accommodation at Charlottes Pass and six of us headed down: Phil, Dan, Sharna, Carley, myself, and Phil's son Craig, who drove himself. It felt like a long-awaited chance to do something just for us, away from the constant decision-making and stress. There was a lot of excitement in the car as we hoped for plenty of snow during our trip.

We rented skis, poles, jackets, pants, and other gear, and I had arranged lessons for all of us. However, Dan, being impatient and eager, wanted to snowboard instead of ski. So, we fitted him out and I suggested he go and familiarise himself with the small slope before his lesson at 1:30pm, while the rest of us got geared up.

When Phil, Sharna, Carley, and I were ready, Dan met us and announced that he had already taken two rides up the chairlift. He did not proceed with a lesson, but the rest of us went ahead with ours. I was amazed by Dan's natural ability for snowboarding, especially considering he had never seen snow before.

I had imagined he might pursue a job at the snow fields during the winter months, but he never did.

We had a wonderful five days with only one knee injury among us. We hardly saw Dan during the day, as he was on the first chairlift up the mountain and only stopped for lunch. He certainly made the most of his time on the slopes and slept like a log each night. Today he still loves snowboarding and tries to go as much as possible. It was such a well-deserved holiday, and we still talk about it.

Teeth

As Bob couldn't chew food and was limited to blended and smooth potions, his teeth began decaying and became very sore. Due to this discomfort, both the nurses and I found it challenging to clean them. It was so painful he would close his mouth and push us away every time we went near them.

We found a Dentist who was prepared to check and clean his teeth. For most people, a trip to the dentist may not seem daunting, but for Bob, it presented some complications. We needed to find a dentist with facilities all on ground level, as Bob's wheelchair was large and bulky. The only dentist available to us was located in an older style house with small rooms and narrow hallways. Manoeuvring his wheelchair through these tight spaces proved to be extremely difficult.

Col arrived with the taxi, so Bob, Liz, and I were all set to see what this day would bring. We needed to travel along Wyong Road, and Bob, busy spelling out messages, pressed the talk button which said, "All these roundabouts are framboozling me". We couldn't understand what he was saying because he wasn't the best speller, and the road was bumpy. After many attempts, we realised he was trying to say, "These roundabouts are bamboozling me". There are about 14 roundabouts on Wyong Road. We were exhausted. The brain was tired before we even got there.

Annie Warren

Just imagine it:

He can't be transferred into the dentist's chair, so we had to juggle his chair beside it.

He cannot open his mouth very wide.

He cannot have water or the water drill as he will choke.

His teeth were in such a bad state; it was going to be too big a job to do in the surgery. But the dentist said he would take out the main two teeth causing discomfort.

We booked another appointment for the next week, where we went through it all again. The appointment was for 1 hour, being such a difficult job, so we arrived on time and went straight in. Bob wanted to talk to the dentist, but the dentist was getting a bit stressed and needed to move on with the job. Time is precious, and there were more patients to see.

Bob had different ideas, and every time we took his board away, he would bang on his table, wanting to say something. Everyone tried to explain to Bob that the Dentist needed to get to work, however there was no reasoning as he had an important message to ask the dentist, so we gave the board back to him. He spelt out, "How do I know you are qualified to work on my teeth?" Then he looked at the dentist with a very inquisitive look on his face.

The poor dentist was gobsmacked; he had never been asked that before. His face showed frustration, shock, and confusion. Not knowing what to say, he went to the wall, grabbed his framed certificates, and put them in front of Bob, saying, "Will this do?"

Bob gave him the thumbs up, laughed, sat back, and opened his mouth as wide as he could. Two molars were removed that day.

When is my Daddy Coming Home

We wheeled him out of the surgery, with a large rolled swab protruding from each side of his mouth, and he appeared very pleased with himself. We had to ensure that the blood did not enter his lungs.

The dentist recommended that we admit him to the hospital to remove the remaining teeth. I believe the dentist really earned his money that day and didn't want to see us again. I don't think he, Liz or I could go through that experience again either, it was so draining.

We always relied on the disabled taxi whenever we took Bob out. They were incredibly patient and accommodating with Bob, and we never had to wait long for them to arrive. They were familiar with us, so a simple phone call and they would turn up promptly. It was truly an excellent service.

The hospital visit was much smoother for all of us. However, as he waited to be put under anaesthetic, Bob noticed a motorbike helmet in the room. Before going into the operating theatre, he insisted on knowing who it belonged to.

Whenever Bob wanted to communicate something, there was no moving forward until he had typed it all out. So, when the surgeon confessed the motorbike helmet was his, Bob inquired about the type of bike he rode, wondering if it was a Harley. He mentioned he once used to ride a Harley himself. This sparked a lively conversation involving all the doctors and Bob was ecstatic! I could only shake my head and laugh.

Bob had never owned a Harley, but it had always been his dream. He had a way of being convincing, even with his severe brain injury, and people would believe his stories. How could you walk away from someone like that, he entertained me so often.

His gums healed well, and he returned to his usual self with relatively few issues - minus all his teeth, of course. Thankfully, there was never any mention of him needing dentures. That would have been another headache. Just imagine where they might end up, how many times he might lose them, or even worse, swallow them. We already had enough trouble with his TV remote constantly disappearing.

Sydney 2000 Olympics - The Torch Relay

What a wonderful time it was, watching people pass the Olympic torch as they journeyed through every town in Australia. The anticipation grew as they approached our own town. Bob was particularly excited because they were going to pass within a street of the Nursing Home.

He was dressed nicely, and we attached the Aussie flag to his wheelchair and we wheeled him down to the corner where they would pass by. There were many people gathered, and we had secured a great spot. However, some individuals thought it was acceptable to stand in front of the wheelchair. When they realised, they would move, but more would take their place. Bob grew increasingly angry and frustrated, but they didn't seem to care.

We were on a four-lane road with a central island, so we decided to take Bob to the middle of the road and place him on the island where no one could obstruct his view. He was incredibly excited and felt immensely proud.

As the runners approached, the handover took place right in front of him. The excitement he displayed was amazing. He smiled, laughed, pointed at the runners, coughed until he would go red in the face.

When a runner approached him, they asked for his name and placed the torch in his hand. It was a wonderful moment, and the expression on his face said it all.

Later, I asked him what it felt like to hold the Olympic torch.

His response was, "I thought I had just competed in a marathon." He was on a high for days, eagerly watching as many races and events as he could. He proudly told the nurses and anyone who visited that he was a very fast runner in his youth and he thought he might make it to the Olympics one day. Perhaps only in his dreams, ha ha! It didn't take much to bring him joy.

Bob's Story as Told to His Carer in His Words.

"My name is Bob and I was born on the 19th of July 1944 in Wangaratta, which is near Ballarat in Queensland, to a dairy farmer. I have many memories of my past that I would like to share with you.

When I was 19 years old I worked as a shearer. I was known as a gun shearer because one day I sheared 246 sheep in a day, during that time I also became known as ratbag, this term has followed me well in the future and is still with me today.

My father also grew up in Wangaratta and was known as the son of a dairy farmer.

As a family man he managed a 5,000 acre sheep property and employed 3 families to help him. An Irishman by the name of Brown and an Australian named Kilfoil. There were 12,000 sheep, 600 cattle and my brothers' racehorses on this property.

Once my brother's horse won a race at Ballarat. Its name was Fabian. Fabian was a galloper in a Melbourne Cup race. In this race he won a cup and 2,000 pounds, which was a lot of money in those days. He won prizes on other occasions, but the 2,000 pounds was the most he ever won, the smallest I remember was 10 pounds.

My brother's name was Ernie, he was also a good shearer and now has his own sheep station. At one stage I had an interest in Bee's and kept 5 hives. My mother never had to buy honey while on the farm.

Mum used to dabble in bird keeping, I think I was about 11 years old. She had about 5 budgies, quails and parrots. They used to squawk so I would go crook on them. My Mum's name was Mylie and my fathers was Jim.

When I was 12, I went to a school called Monivea College just outside of Bray. Prior to this I went to Skipton Primary School. I don't think they liked me too much. I reckon they had a public holiday when I left.

I was a pretty good athlete and won heaps of medals and certificates.

My dad used to say I was a bum because I rode a motorbike, but they were good for rounding up the sheep and giving my Mum the shits.

I met Annie when I was 14 years old. Her family had a farm within five miles of our property, but our relationship did not get serious until I was 17. I prayed to God that she was the right one and I think he did not let me down. Annie and I got married in a Catholic Church in Skipton. It cost me an arm and a leg because the priest was so surprised to see me in a church.

My best man was my brother Ernie and Annie's bridesmaids were her sisters Carmel and Mary. I wore a brown suit and so did my brother, Annie wore a traditional white gown and her bridesmaids wore pink. I reckon they were rushed off their feet by all the blokes.

The reception was at home so they wouldn't have to carry me too far in case I got drunk, but I never did because Annie would have left me, she had a good head on her shoulders.

When is my Daddy Coming Home

Our first child was born fifteen months later, a son who we named Daniel, but I wanted to call him Otis, but Annie didn't like that name. I was so proud; he was a beautiful little boy. Then later we had a daughter and named her Sharna, she was so beautiful.

At the time I was working as a station hand and we had a great vegie garden. We never had to buy very much. Once I won a prize in a show for the best cauliflower."

And that was Bob's story. He was incredibly creative. I think he got so caught up in his own tales that he actually believed them himself.

I had some good laughs. Many times when doctors, psychiatrists, Insurance doctors or anyone came to assess him, they would walk away shaking their heads as he was so convincing with his stories.

For a start, I didn't meet him until he was 30, and I was 21. I've never lived on a sheep farm and we met in Mt Isa where he was working in the mines. My bridesmaids were my girlfriends and they wore Green, and we were married in the Presbyterian church at Toukley. It was never dull going to visit him as we never knew what story he would tell us that day.

Paul Hogan

Another time the carer and Bob wrote to Paul Hogan

To Mr. Paul Hogan
Crocodile Dundee

Dear Mr. Hogan,

> My name is Bob Warren, and I am writing to ask for an autographed picture of yourself. I think you are a True-Blue Australian Hero.
>
> I don't think I have missed one of your movies in the last 10 years.
>
> My wife said to me if I didn't bullshit so much I'd be just like you.
>
> I have been in a wheelchair with quadriplegia and acquired brain injury for thirteen years. I was 44 when I was a passenger in a car accident on my way to work in Bowen, North Queensland.
>
> Your movies make me feel that I'm not in a wheelchair, I feel alive again. Before the accident I would go pig shooting in Northern QLD and when I was young I would go in the Western District of Victoria. My nickname was Nit Nat Have a Chat Beer Bottle Bob. I still have my Akubra hat that I used to wear, and it has seven crocodile teeth in the hatband. I am wearing it in the picture that I have enclosed.

When is my Daddy Coming Home

My favourite movies that you have made are Crocodile Dundee 1 and 2 and I own them both and watch them every week.

God Bless you Paul and God Bless your lovely family.

I also have a family that I am very proud of, my wife Annie and our two children Dan and Sharna.

I hear you are making Crocodile Dundee 3 so I will look forward to watching that one.

All the best mate, I hope you don't mind that I have called you a mate.

From Bob Warren.

The note at the bottom of the letter was from his carer, which read…

"Bob loves your movies so much and he thinks he is you catching that crocodile. He will ask every day when I am leaving to watch it. He is totally dependent on carers but never complains and has such a wicked sense of humour. You can't feel sad around him.

We, as carers, thought it would be lovely to write to you and let you know how much pleasure your movies have given to this wonderful man. You would certainly make him a very happy person if you could just send a photo signed by yourself."

So, we sent the photo of Bob with his hat with the crocodile teeth and the letter to Paul Hogan and waited patiently for a photo. It never came, no response at all, we were all very disappointed, but Bob kept watching his favourite movies every day.

Bob would spell out messages every day, often repeating himself without realising it. His communication device was an old model, but it worked well for him. We had attempted to introduce more modern boards, but his limited, jerky movements with his right hand made it very frustrating for him to operate. Once he became accustomed to the Real Voice device, there was no stopping him from chatting, unless the nurses forgot to charge it overnight. Frustratingly, another recurring issue was that it wouldn't turn on and we would have to send it away for repairs.

Here are a few more of his amusing messages:

> "I think the wonderful nurses should get danger money and a very big pay rise for looking after Ratbag Bob."

> "Are you one of the many casualties of Ratty Bob's sense of humour?"

> "Hail Mary full of grace the lord is with you, if you have been good."

> "I am a ratbag, and I am shocked that this talking machine knows it."

> "I pray to the good lord that Dan and Sharna don't turn out like me. If they do, God help us all."

> "I wouldn't tell you a fib, where would I get my chocolates from, just tell me that?"

> "If I had an electric wheelchair, I would be the only person in Australia to have a bloody bulbar on it. I would give all the old ladies the bloody shits in the hospital and probably get thrown out."

> "You told me on Monday that you woke up from a dream and said how did I get such a gorgeous hunk of a man"

> "I wish I wasn't such a bloody burden on you."

When is my Daddy Coming Home

"You should get danger money for putting up with bullshit Bob or a gold medal for putting your life in danger by listening to my chats or is it too late have you been overcome by Bob's body fumes you poor nurses."

"I've had no success with this talking machine until I called myself a ratbag, when I told a lie it called me a bloody ratbag. Fair Dinkum!!"

He always had a lot to say and would keep you there as long as he could. Then he would go into gaga land and forget you had been to visit. His brain injury was so difficult at times and then there were times when he was so on the ball, you forgot he had a brain injury. It was hard to wrap your head around it all.

Sharna and I took Bob for a walk one day and bumped into a lady, Margaret, and her son Jack, whom we had met through the CASS group. Jack also had an acquired brain injury. While I was talking to Margaret, Bob had noticed that Jack had an electric wheelchair. Bob would love to have one. He was asking the young man about it, "how fast does it go", and "have you done a wheelie in it?"

Jack could talk, albeit with very slurred speech, and he answered all of Bob's questions.

"No, I haven't done any wheelies," Jack replied. Bob inquired further, "Have you been to the pub down the road?" Jack responded, "No, I am not allowed to drink."

Bob is spelling out all these messages and speaking them on his machine, which talks in an American accent. It was working overtime with Bob's questions.

Bob: "Do you smoke?"
Jack: "No, I can't smoke."

Then Bob says, "You're not the full quid, are you?" He keeps his finger on the talk button so it repeats over and over again. Poor Sharna was trying to pull his hand away and turn the machine off. Bob was laughing so hard and ended up having a coughing fit. Sharna and I were horrified and so embarrassed.

When the State of Origin was on, he would get so excited because he loved football. He enjoyed making a bet with Phil that QLD would win, and they would seal the deal with a shake on a bottle of Chivas Regal.

However, when NSW won and Phil went to visit him, Bob would spell out, "I bought you a bottle of Chivas Regal, but I drank my half, which just happened to be on the bottom, so I had to drink your half to get to mine." Then he would look at Phil to gauge his reaction, tilt his head, and burst into laughter.

The Rocky Road of Brain Injuries

We felt incredibly blessed that Bob was left with his sense of humour and personality following the accident. Despite his injuries, he remained unaware of the extent of his condition or the duration of his time in a coma, hospital, nursing home, and inability to speak or eat.

It's remarkable how different individuals with similar injuries can undergo identical treatments - surgeries, medication, drugs, and therapy - and yet achieve varied outcomes. The brain is often likened to a computer, and repairing its damaged 'wires' can be exceedingly challenging.

Bob seemed to approach each day as it came, finding happiness in the company of visitors, even though he wouldn't retain memories of their presence. I believe it's often tougher on the family caring for someone with an Acquired Brain Injury, as they grapple with their own thoughts and uncertainties about the future.

There were numerous times when we were called to the Nursing Home or Hospital due to various health challenges Bob faced - such as infections like MRSA, Cellulitis, pneumonia, severe flu, pressure sores, or critical decisions regarding another operation. It's hard to count the number of times we had to bid our farewells to him as he was deemed to be on the brink of passing away, with doctors stating that he couldn't bounce back from this one. However, let me tell you, the will to live within this extraordinary man surpassed everyone's expectations. Why? That was a question we were still trying to figure out.

The list of medical challenges seemed never-ending, and each time the doctors would call me, asking if I wanted them to continue treating him or to let him go. Who was I to make such a serious decision about whether he should live or die? Yes, I was his wife, but he had fought so hard for so long. I felt as though I was playing with his life.

Sometimes, I'd receive these calls from the doctors while driving along the busy freeway, with B-Double trucks whizzing past, or while juggling the responsibilities of caring for two young kids at home. Other times, I could be at work, trying to earn a living, or simply out shopping. In those moments, Liz, Max, Phil, and I would convene for a roundtable meeting, finding peace in our collective thoughts and perspectives.

Still, the weight of the decision ultimately fell upon me, and I constantly grappled with the feeling that I was once again playing with his life. It was a harrowing experience, to say the least.

We knew, in his own way, he was happy, in his twisted, contorted body. Thankfully he was left with the same cheeky personality that he always had. He would see people in wheelchairs, nowhere near as disabled as himself, and he would write a message about the poor bugger, how sorry he felt for them. We would just shake our heads. Thankfully with the brain injury Bob had, he had no idea how disabled and incapacitated he was.

One of Bob's doctors once confided in me that they had learned a great deal from treating Bob's brain injury and quadriplegia. Initially, they hadn't realised that he could find happiness or have any quality of life in his condition. However, as the years passed, they came to know and understand Bob better. Through treating him during his sickest moments, even when he was at the brink of death, they gradually realised that he did indeed have a quality of life. They reached a point where they never had to ask me again whether to continue treating him or not. They had gained invaluable insights from him as their patient.

Last Days

During one of Liz and my usual Wednesday visits, Bob appeared to be in a lot of pain and was unresponsive to our efforts to make him more comfortable. We had seen him like this many times before, so we weren't overly concerned.

We asked the nurses, when they had a spare minute, to put him back to bed. That's when I noticed the rash on his stomach and was told, "that's just a heat rash." When they took a better look, they exclaimed, "Ohhhh, that wasn't there this morning when we showered and dressed him." But it certainly looked aggressive now. Bob was not his usual self and seemed to be in a lot of pain. He wasn't interested in watching TV or a movie or even chatting. We knew something was wrong.

I asked them to call his doctor and keep me informed about what was happening.

After 2 days, they rang to say it was Cellulitis. He had high temperatures and his breathing was erratic; he needed to go to the hospital. He was a very sick fellow. For the next few days, we took turns sitting with him at the hospital. I rang work and said I can't come in because Bob was really sick. They were fantastic.

Bob wasn't responding to visitors, medication, doctors, or anything we tried. We would ring people so he could hear their voices, but to no avail. Then, each night, he got worse, and for four nights, I would get a phone call around 10:45pm to come in.

I would pick Liz up, and off we would go to Wyong Hospital, sitting for hours not knowing what was going on. His stomach was expanding, and the rash was becoming more aggressive. I had rung both the kids, who by this stage were in their early 30s and had their own lives.

Dan came and stayed each night. Sharna and her 6-month-old identical twin boys also came from Sydney. That was a full-time job in itself, but somehow we juggled it all. It was a very difficult time; Bob wasn't responding to the medication or any treatment. We didn't know what to tell everyone. It was like he was comatose once again.

We sent for Roslyn, Bob's sister, to come from Victoria. Bob had been similar to this many times, but he always seemed to respond to the treatment. This time was different. He was starting to really concern me now.

Roslyn caught a flight the next day, arriving at Newcastle Airport, but could only get a late flight at 9:30pm. Dan and Sharna went to Newcastle to pick her up, while Phil and I stayed home with these beautiful twins and also in case the hospital rang.

Her flight was delayed by an hour or so, when once again I received the dreaded phone call to say I needed to get to the hospital. Every night at the same time, 10:45pm. So, leaving Phil with the twins, off I went, hoping they wouldn't wake up.

Bob, still not responding to treatment, had an upper respiratory infection and Cellulitis around his peg site. I didn't ring Liz this time, as she had been coming down every night, and I had seen Bob a lot sicker at other times. Knowing Roslyn was on her way and could take the pressure off Liz, who had been so supportive, leaving Max every night to come with me, sitting for ages and not being able to help or do anything to make him more comfortable.

I rang Dan and told him to come straight to the hospital with Ros and Sharna. They were in my car, a little more comfortable and with plenty of fuel, so I took Sharna's car to the hospital, only to have the oil light come on halfway there.

I arrived at 11:15pm to see flashing red and blue fire engine lights surrounding the hospital. When I went to the reception, they informed me to go straight to his room where they were waiting for us. It was on the 4th floor, and because there may have been a fire, the elevators were not to be used. It was scary going through those corridors on my own at that time of night, thinking there was a fire somewhere.

A hospital looks so different in the quiet of the night. I had no idea where I was going as so many corridors had been shut off. I must admit I was quite terrified. When I arrived at Bob's room, he had just passed; I was too late that night. Dan, Sharna, Ros, and I all said our goodbyes with many tears, feeling so sorry for Ros. If her plane was on time, maybe she may have had a moment with Bob before he passed.

The nurse said she had been with him and just stepped out when she heard the fire alarms start to go off. It's quite freaky, but the alarms started in that room, and yes, I can see him going out pressing all the buttons!

There never was any fire.

At long last, on the 28th of February 2011, he was at peace after 23 years. How he survived is beyond me, with the injuries, operations, and the number of times we were called to his bedside and told he was dying. The toxins being produced in his body - he simply could not survive. But he did! There were many possible reasons why:

- He needed to see his kids grow up, to become young adults.
- He wanted to become a grandfather.
- He just hung around to wind me up and make my life hell.
- Maybe it just wasn't his time yet.

Whatever the reason, he amazed many people with his will to live, determination, strength, and attitude. Now, it was time to give him the send-off he truly deserved.

The Funeral

People started arriving from Townsville, Victoria, and Port Macquarie. The night before the funeral, friends and family were all gathered on our front porch when someone asked me what was on top of Sharna and Shane's car. I had just finished preparing and writing out the eulogy, so I was quite stressed, tired, and exhausted. The car was parked on the front lawn and had a pod on the roof. I happened to say, "that's the coffin - Bob's in there," then there was silence. I added, "You don't think he's going to miss this party, do you?"

Everyone broke out into laughter, with the neighbours coming over to see what the commotion was about. So then they joined us also. Everyone had some funny stories to tell about Bob Warren. He would have loved it.

We didn't anticipate a very large funeral, considering it had been 23 years since his accident, and most of his mates now lived away or had not been in contact for many years. So I was very surprised to see the room filling up. There were nurses, doctors, Camp Breakaway volunteers, The Bowling Ladies, staff from the Nursing Home, The CASS group, and some colleagues from my work. Additionally, now that the kids had grown up and had their own family and friends, they were there to support Dan and Sharna. There were all our family members and friends from our lives back in Townsville before the accident were also present.

When is my Daddy Coming Home

Most of the people there hadn't known Bob before his accident, so we wanted to show them what a fun-loving husband, father, and friend he was. How he loved his veggie garden, fishing, his Collingwood team, having a beer with his mates, and touch football. We made a photo slideshow with him and the kids, wrestling when they were little, on the motorbike with our special dog Kina, sliding down the natural rock water slides just north of Townsville, fishing, and holidaying in our tent on Whitsunday Island, dressing up for the kids, and just being a fun dad.

I was so happy with the send-off we gave him. He would have loved it, and wondered what the fuss was all about. We played his favourite song, True Blue, and certainly celebrated his life, telling stories, lies, bullshit, having quite a few ales, laughing, dancing, hugging and crying. He would have loved to see us all there for him.

After 23 years it had come to an end. No more doctors, operations, Wednesday and Saturday visits, my life had been so occupied by organising his, that I felt lost now, with so much more time on my hands. It was a very strange feeling. It was time for Phil and I to start our journey, retire and enjoy our new life together.

It's now been 36 years since that dreadful day which changed our lives forever.

Writing this story has been very emotional, depressing, therapeutic and inspiring. If it helps just one person by reading it, then what I set out to achieve has paid off. I had no idea what I was doing, or who to go to for help or advice. But after seeing the smile on Bob's face every time we visited, I believe we did a pretty good job.

Today, Dan and Mel are approaching their second wedding anniversary. I am so pleased for them both. Everybody needs to find happiness. They have two beautiful girls, Airlie, 10 years old and Ocea 7. Sharna and Shane are engaged. You can't rush some things, the twins - Callum and Hunter are now 14, and Ryder is 12.

Phil and I are happy and enjoying our retired life. He loves his golf, and I simply appreciate every day with walks and swims at the beach, with my treasured sister Liz. Phil and I are also engaged but feel we are already married. We love to travel in our van and realise how precious life is.

Sadly, my brother-in-law Max passed away on the October long weekend 2022. He was a wonderful support for the kids and I, never questioning my decisions, letting us live with them for nearly 3 years, and helping so much with Bob. He is very much missed.

Phil's three children, Brett, Craig and Carley have always been supportive and helpful around Bob and lovely towards me. We have four of the five kids living within 10km of us. We now have 13 grandkids, and it can be crazy when we are all together, but we love every minute.

This is my story.
Annie Warren

Bob's Eulogy

Written by Sharna Warren, March 2011

Bob, Bobby, Ratbag Bob, Bullshit Bob, Nit Nat Have a Chat Beer Bottle Bob, Didyabringyabeeralong, Bobette, Roberty Bob, Bobby Poo, Mr Bob, Dad, and most recently, Poppy Old Fart. He may have had a lot of aliases, but I reckon my dad was a fair dinkum, true blue, bloke.

We had a lot of fun with Dad - camping up the mountains or on the Whitsundays Islands, fishing, collecting minis - yes the cars - Mum was so impressed, painting cartoon characters on the chook shed and the water tank, playing minute mime, cards and Scrabble. He'd always win, but he always cheated.

Dad was very artistic and creative, he could draw anything and always wrote little poems for us to take to school, like 'Ants in ya Pants' or 'Chooks'. The teachers were never impressed.

All our chooks had names, but Dad's fav by far was Red, a huge Rooster who mum hated. He woke her every morning and would even charged her in the car with Dad shouting out to watch his precious mate.

In the end, he did taste good!

After Dad's accident he was no longer able to speak, but where there's a will, there's a way. And for old Have a Chat, we managed to find a special keyboard that could spell out his message and when he hit the return key it would speak his message in a funny American accent.

One time we took Dad out and bumped into a lady and her son, who was in a motorised wheelchair. As Mum was chatting to the lady, Dad was asking the fella if he could do wheelies, doughnuts, etc. then looks at me and spells out 'he's not the full quid', leaving his finger on the return button to repeat the message over and over. You never knew what the cheeky bugger was going to say.

My greatest pleasure was introducing my boys Callum and Hunter to their Poppy Old Fart. Every week, for about three months, he told the nurses I'd had the babies. Two girls; a boy and a girl; two boys. He was always so convincing and always had names - Anne and Annette, Andy & Andrew and believe it or not, even Anne and Bob! When they did finally arrive, he just adored them so much his whole face would light up.

Dad has taught us so much. He had the strongest mind and the most incredible will to live. He had such passion for life. He taught us to appreciate life to the max, don't take anyone or anything for granted.

Everyone has a story, so pick your head up, put a smile on your face, have a laugh and don't take life so seriously. Bob never did.

Chooks

Written by Bob Warren in the 80s

Chooks! Those Ruddy Chooks

Cause all types of trouble

All them chooks

Scratch here and scratch there

Scratch up mother's garden

You should hear her go crook

Over all them ruddy chooks

You should have seen her look

When that Rooster crows

Before the crack of dawn

3 o'clock or was it four in the morn

Mum turns over in bed and gives a big yawn

Said one day I will fix that lot

I will put them all in the pot

We will invite everyone for chicken broth

Ruddy Chooks! That will fix the ruddy lot.

Acknowledgments

Writing this book has been a journey I never imagined I would be able to achieve, yet it is mine, encapsulating 23 years of caregiving and navigating the complexities of another's life. I am deeply grateful for the support of my family and friends who cheered me on throughout this endeavour. Without their encouragement, this book would have remained untold.

To Liz, you sacrificed your time, your home and your family on countless occasions to help me through all the hard moments and critical decisions I had to make, and there were so many. Your support, love and care held no boundaries. You and Max were my lifeline to keep going, for myself, and for my two kids. What a beautiful sister you are. Sadly, Max has passed, although I'll be forever grateful for what he and Liz did for me.

To Phil, you have always been by my side, and your companionship has been a tower of strength and comfort in my toughest days. You never questioned my decisions and encouraged me all the way. The challenges we faced made us all the more stronger.

To Dan and Sharna, thank you for your understanding and empathy towards the necessity of this book; you were both so young and I felt it was important for you both to have the opportunity to comprehend the journey your father took to watch you grow up.

Sharna - I appreciate your contribution helping me bring my story together into its present form.

To Kim Wright, Robbie Croatto, Estelle and Robyn - your friendship, help and guidance in those early days were lifelines that kept me afloat. I am forever grateful for your unwavering support and encouragement. I can't imagine where I'd be without you all by my side.

To my family members, your consistent interest and assistance throughout Bob's life was invaluable. Your love and support has been an endless source of strength and motivation through some extremely tough times.

Special thanks to Helene Bradshaw, whose advice and encouragement on my story have been invaluable. Your guidance has helped shape this story into what it is today.

Bob and me on our Wedding Day 1975

Bob, his sister Roslyn, Me and Roslyn's Husband Kevin 1975

Bob fishing 1975

Bob and me 1975

Bob preparing a Hangi for our 10th wedding anniversary 1985

Bob, Dan, Kina and a stray puppy 1979

Bob, Dan and Sharna 1983

Me, Sharna and Bob on Magnetic Island 1980

Bob teaching Dan to shear a sheep 1984

Dan, Bob, Robert and Robbie near Rollingstone NQ

Bob's 43rd birthday 1987

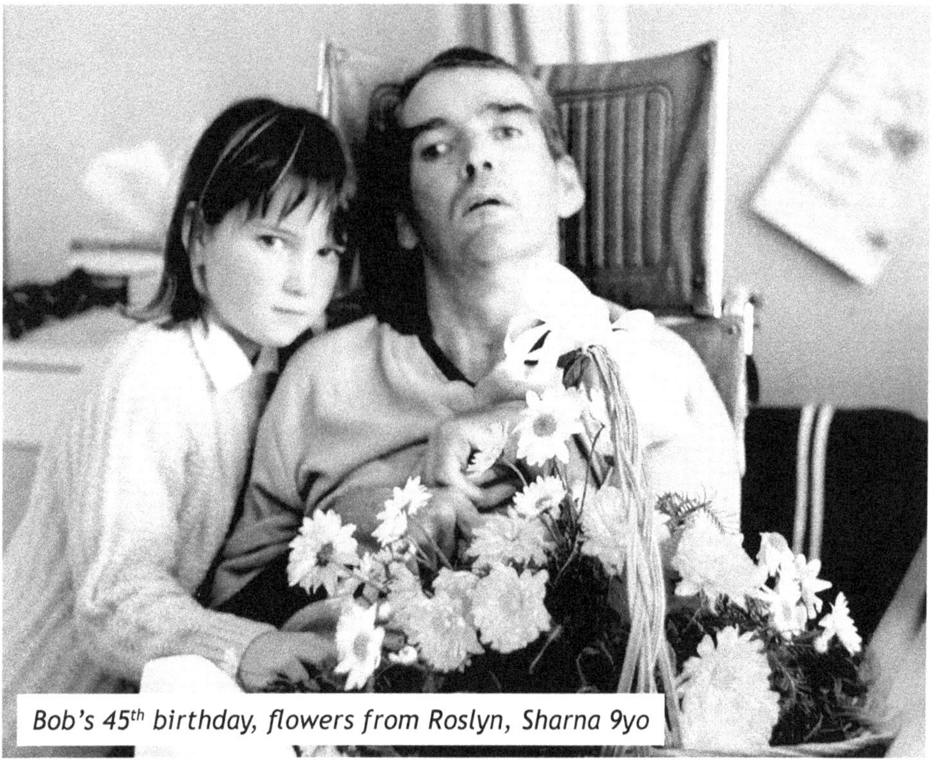

Bob's 45th birthday, flowers from Roslyn, Sharna 9yo

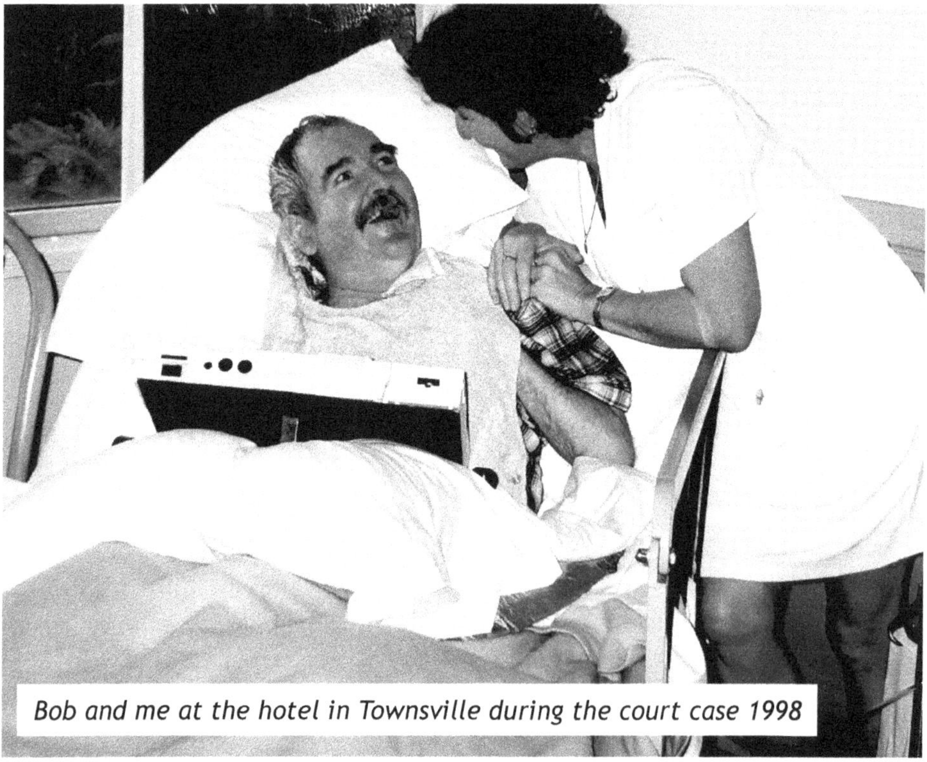

Bob and me at the hotel in Townsville during the court case 1998

Liz and Bob at the nursing home

Friends visiting from Townsville: Robert, Bob, Anthony, Pete and Robbie

Kim visiting from Giru

Bob, Christie and Pete in Townsville

Jack, Bob, Jimmy and Agnes

Bob and Beth

Bob taking a Harley ride at Camp Breakaway

Bob sailing at Camp Breakaway

Christmas at Liz's

Christmas at Brian's

The kids from Giru – trip back to visit in 1989

The crew in Townsville for the Court Case – 1998

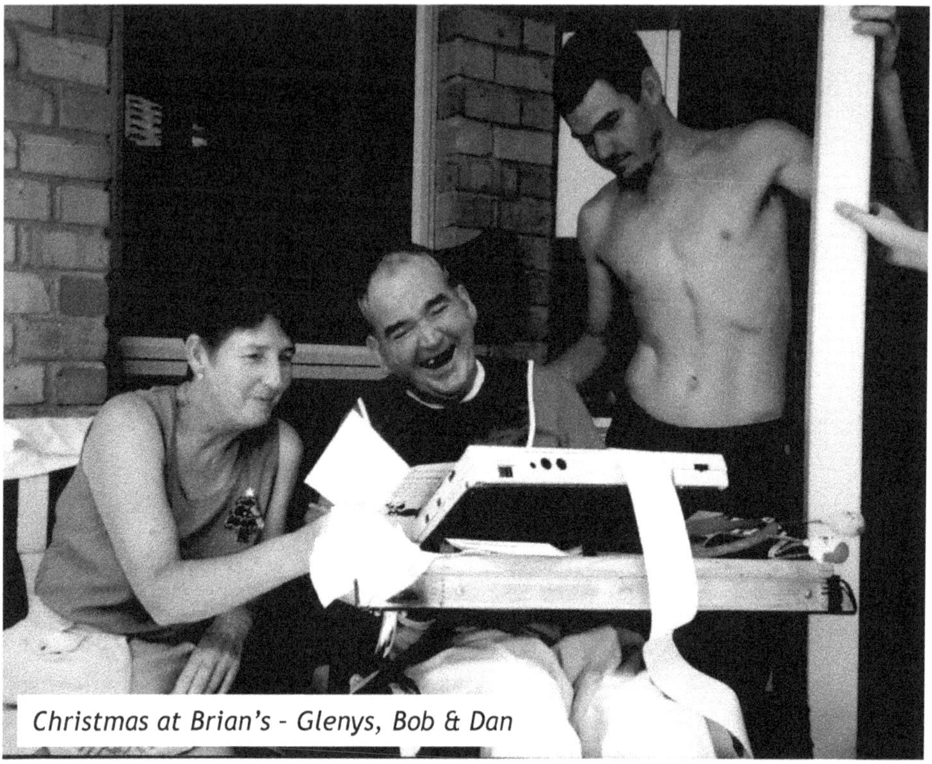

Christmas at Brian's – Glenys, Bob & Dan

Christmas at Brian's – Bob and Brian playing pool

Phil and Bob at Long Jetty

Roslyn and Bob

Bob showing us his best Crocodile Dundee impersonation.

Bob with the Sydney 2000 Olympic Torch

Dan and Bob

Sharna and Bob

Sharna, Callum, Poppy Bob, Hunter and Shane

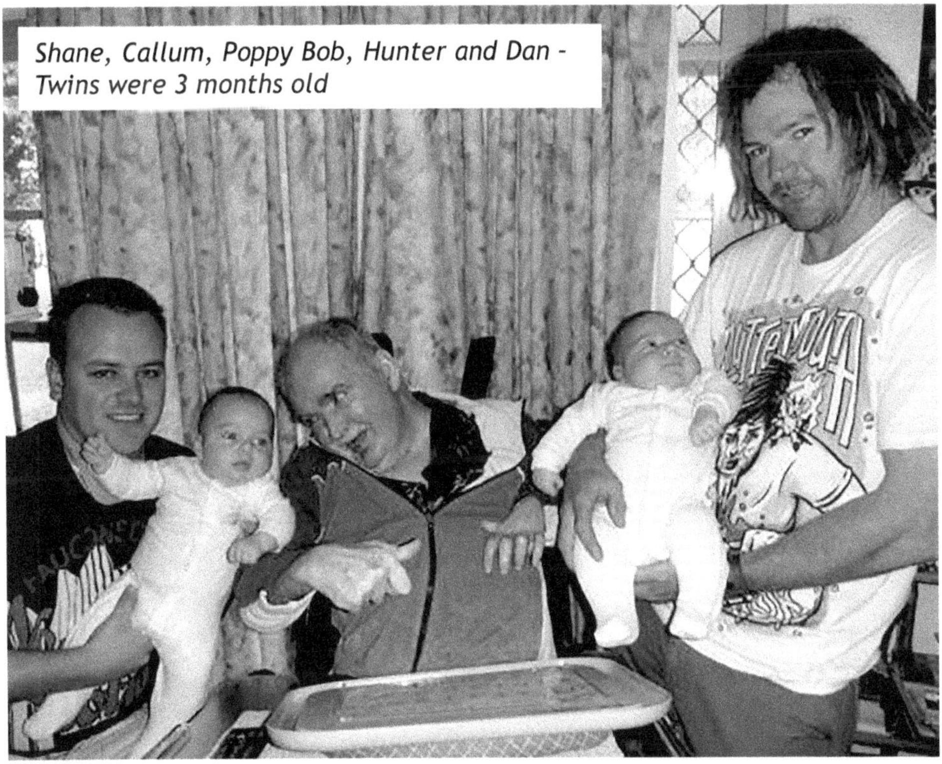

Shane, Callum, Poppy Bob, Hunter and Dan – Twins were 3 months old

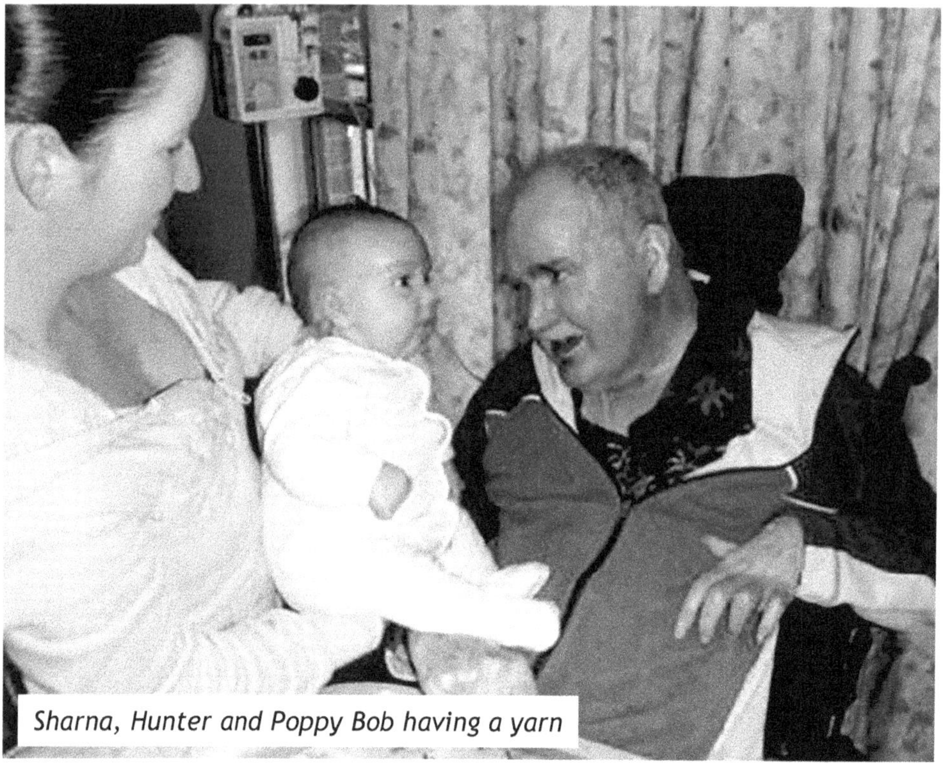

Sharna, Hunter and Poppy Bob having a yarn

Poppy Bob giving Callum a kiss

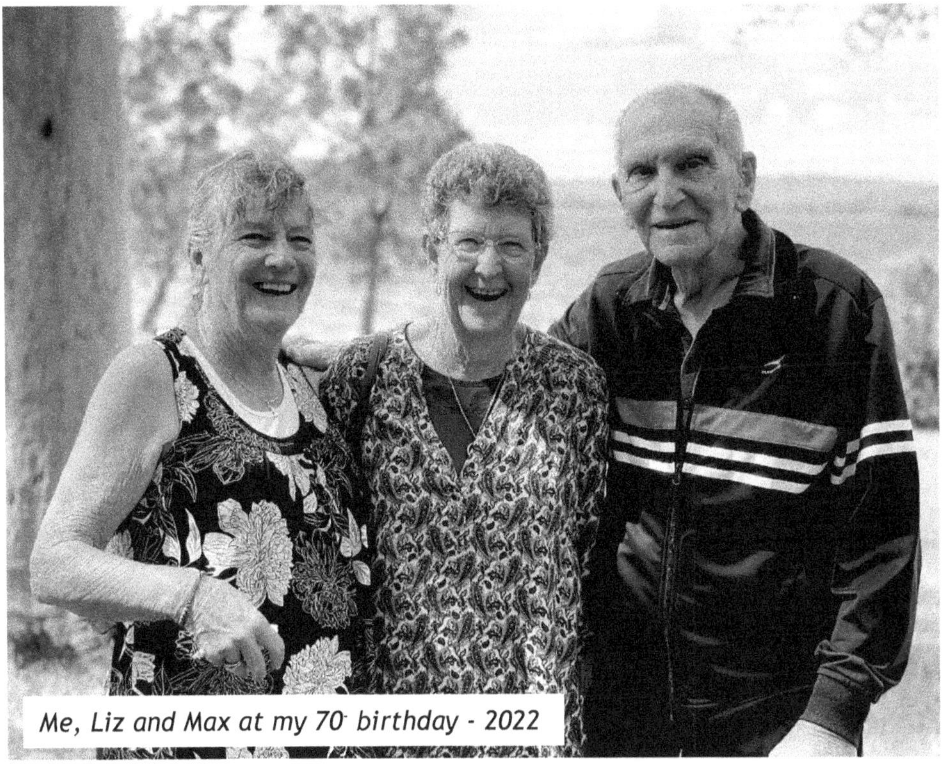

Me, Liz and Max at my 70 birthday - 2022

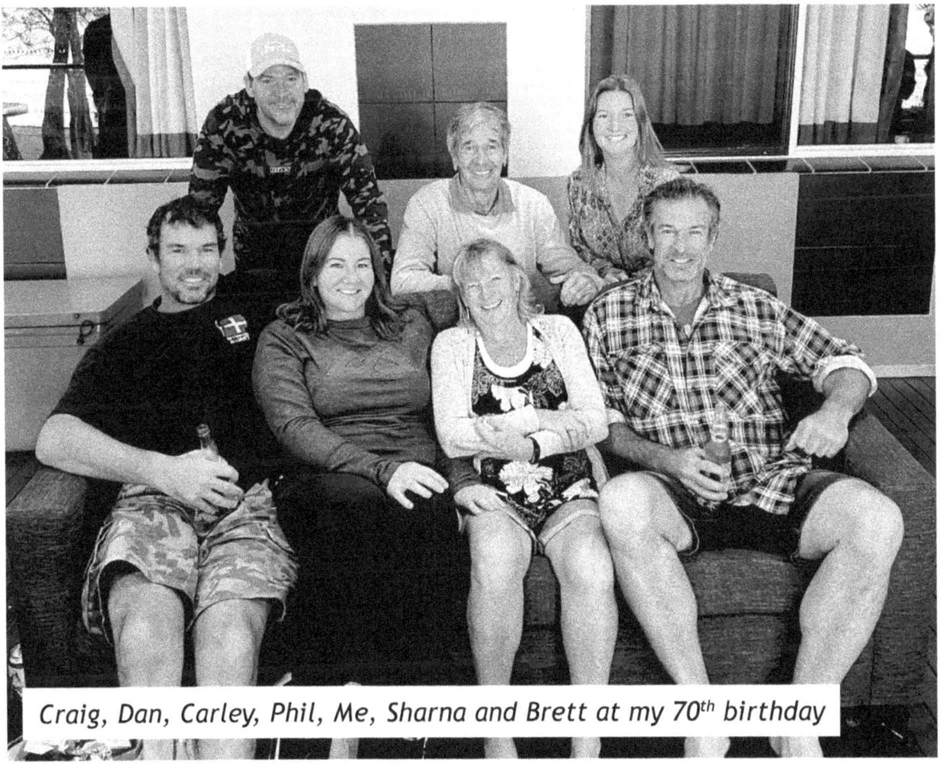

Craig, Dan, Carley, Phil, Me, Sharna and Brett at my 70th birthday

Hunter, Shane, Ryder, Phil, Callum, Ocea, Mel, Dan, Airlie, Me and Sharna – 2022

Family and friends celebrating my 70th birthday – 2022

www.ingramcontent.com/pod-product-compliance
Lightning Source LLC
Chambersburg PA
CBHW041145110526
44590CB00027B/4131